The
BITCH'S
GUIDE to
HANDLING MEN

Also by Tony Fennelly

The Glory Hole Murders
The Closet Hanging
Kiss Yourself Goodbye
The Hippie in the Wall
1-900-Dead
Don't Blame the Snake
Home Dead for Christmas

The
BITCH'S
GUIDE to
HANDLING MEN

Tony Fennelly

INTRODUCTION: Why You Need This Book

You may meet your ideal man in a trendy nightclub or at a large social affair. He's not exactly handsome, you decide, but appealing in his own way. Over an evening of drinks and finger foods, "Mr. Wonderful" reveals that he is a lawyer on the partnership track at one of the prestigious firms in town, has a summer place on Martha's Vineyard, and flies there in his own plane. He loves your smile and your sense of humor. He has never met anyone quite like you, so brilliant and yet so real. Something really special happened to him tonight.

So you convey him back to your apartment on a monsoon of serendipitous passion and spend the whole night in glorious lovemaking. The next day, you dance into work, declaring that all your nights on the depressing singles scene and fruitless dating are over. Your co-workers envy you for capturing this prince of eligible bachelors. You sing at your desk and keep your phone on and in your pocket all day waiting for him to call with a declaration of love as overwhelming and phenomenal as your own.

But he doesn't call, that day or ever.

You may someday learn that your legal eagle is actually a fast-food worker living with his wife and kids in his mother's basement. If ever confronted about his cruel deception, he would declare that he was only telling you exactly what you wanted to hear and that you enjoyed your "fantasy encounter" as much as he did.

You, my dear, have been purely ripped off. Yet again.

However sophisticated women become, we will always want love, marriage, and children. And we are still preyed upon by men who promise those things then leave us broken-hearted.

This manual instructs today's woman on identifying and dealing with predators, liars, sex addicts, con men, leeches,

1

phonies, and cheap skates. You will also learn how to talk to a man, how to pin him down regarding commitments and get him to spend his money.

In past ages, by the time a woman learned "where it was at", she was already too old to be invited there. But today you can access an arsenal of information and strategies once available only in one's senescence and after years of struggle and exploitation. With humor, of course. We always need that.

With this guide in hand, you will achieve that ever-to-be-envied combination: the wisdom of a decadent and shopworn old trollop (like me) in the body of a lovely and vivacious, charmer in her prime. (You.) This is an advantage no wealth could have purchased in previous eras

"Choosing a man is pretty much a matter of deciding which particular set of disgusting characteristics you're willing to put up with." The Bitch's Almanac

CHAPTER ONE: FIND 'EM

This chapter addresses the off-chance that you want a man and don't already have one.

Firstly, wherever you go in search of your soul mate, be sure that you're dead sober for the quest. Not only does alcohol steal away your judgment, dignity, equilibrium, and good looks, but the more you have to drink, the more likely you are to wake up with Don Rickles's less handsome older brother.

College-age people congregate in "watering holes" to socialize. But don't go to bars to meet men if you're over twenty-four. All you will meet will be the kind of lonely wretches who hang out in bars.

Networking events held by the business community are not good social venues. From a distance, they look like sophisticated parties with soft music, shrimp canapés, and caviar. But the "revelers" are there to make business, not friends. The men don't get drunk and the women don't flirt. Everybody pretends to be having fun while really hustling alarm systems and mutual funds with front-end loads.

Mind you, there is bound to be the occasional sex addict who gets up in the morning determined to find a conquest and spends the rest of the day pursuing that objective: in the coffee shop, the laundromat, the newspaper store, and even the business gathering.

It's possible to meet men at parties but don't attend them solely in that hope. And certainly don't stand in the doorway of your next gathering, pick out the least repulsive among the assemblage and hurl yourself in his direction. Men can smell this kind of desperation and it repels them more surely than a video of a home birthing.

Say you see a rugged-looking man across the tennis court. You've heard that he is single, healthy, charming, well-to-do, and straight. He seems to have everything but you. How to make his inventory complete?

Opening lines *not* to proffer:

"Haven't I seen you somewhere before?"

"I can touch my nose with my tongue."

"Can I play with that a while?"

These are crass.

And for your own sake, don't ask the prospect his zodiac sign. Men don't believe in astrology and think anyone who does is a fluff head. You may say, "Isn't this a great party? I love the paté." or "The city is beautiful this time of year." But keep your hands off the gent. You lose a point if he draws away from your touch. Three if he flinches.

Once you have made your subtle overture, it's his part to follow up on the conversation. If he doesn't, smile and move on. What if he won't have you on a bet? First of all, do *not* take it personally. There is nothing wrong with you and maybe nothing wrong with him. You are simply not his type. Or perhaps he is already involved. Or a pouf. In any case, respect his right to his own preferences. Since he's not attracted to you, you've got no edge on him and you must leave at once. Do *not* continue to hover around in the hope that he will eventually discover something likeable about you. And certainly don't cheapen yourself with an invitation like, "If you ever change your mind, I'll be available."

Be forever upbeat:

"Try the shrimp!"

or "The program starts in a few minutes."

or "Have a great time in the city."

When a man gives you the brush-off, you have to pretend you didn't *notice* you were given the brush-off because you were looking over his shoulder at someone much more exciting.

4

If you spot anyone you know, *that* person can serve as the "more exciting someone." Hustle up to him or her and burble and enthuse: "George!/ Mrs. Goldberg!/ Reverend Bailey! Congratulations on your new job!/ new grandchild!/ great review!"

Almost everyone has something going on that they can be congratulated for.

If you don't see anyone you know, a waiter or a bartender can be the "more exciting someone": "Are you an actor?" (He probably is.) "I go to the theater a lot; I think I've seen you in something!" If, on the off-chance, he *isn't* an actor, you can just say he *looks* like a very-attractive actor you've seen recently.

Any man you talk to must be left with a positive image of you. He may be so impressed with your insouciance and savoir faire that he will introduce you to his stunning younger brother. Or his boss.

Don't quickly target another prospect and make the same pitch, seeming both craven and promiscuous. Instead, get in a delightful conversation with another woman. Or a gay fellow. Or that historic-looking gent who graduated from Notre Dame with your father. (The old fossil probably has the best stories at the party anyway.) Just being caught up in something will make you a heap more interesting than the smoking, drinking, corner-sitter.

If a prospect seems attracted to you, if he smiles and the pupils of his eyes expand, the better to take in the wondrous vision of you, get down to the business of learning about each other. But you must not ask a new acquaintance what he does for a living. First of all, it's rude, in effect, asking how much money he makes. But more important, you should have a chance to evaluate him "bare." That is the man himself, looks and personality. Decide if he's a sweet darling or an intolerable boor before you know whether he's a stock broker or a stock boy. Figure who would make you happier, the spoiled scion of a rich oil family who only comes by when he feels like having

5

sex, or an honest working man who gives you his paychecks. And does your housework.

Does the initiate please you as he stands? Would you choose him as your mate if you met him on a desert island or at Club Med, or some other place where wealth and position aren't factors? If you would, the lucky guy has a shot. If not, take your leave gracefully: "Oh, dear! I've got to find the ladies room." or "Goodie! They've put out the roast beef!" and resume your search elsewhere.

The suitable man can help you with your life plan. You do have a plan, right? You're not just going to keep having sex with all and sundry and see what happens. When we were girls, we all wanted a smart guy with sex appeal. When we get old, we may settle for any gent with good manners and no nasty habits who can fix things around the house.

But at an age somewhere in the middle, the most important thing two people can have is not "chemistry" but agenda-convergence. How can this particular man help you with your plans?

The worthy man will help you with your career, either because it jibes with his own: say, you're an actress and he's a director, or he just wants to make you happy, say you're an actress and he's a taxi driver who pays for your headshots and acting lessons. The man you choose must be honest, hard-working, and, most important, love you to distraction. You deserve no less.

Once you have decided that you like a man, it's time to find out how much money he makes. This should be done with appropriate sneakiness.

Ask, "Do you work in the city? (This neighborhood? This building?)"

If he doesn't use that opening to specify his occupation then, either he's ashamed of it or he doesn't think you important enough to inform. An acceptable answer would be "Yeah. I work at Finley Corp. I'm an accountant."

The next day, you can go down to Finley Corp. and apply

for his job. Ask the starting salary and the schedule of raises.

If the man is a government employee, his salary is a matter of public record. Look it up. Should he have his own business, put yourself in the position of a prospective client.

"How much would you charge me to train my horse?"

If you let a new acquaintance know you're attracted to him in the hope of starting a romance, he may assume that you are willing to put out immediately for nothing. So convey your interest in a way that is completely nonsexual. Don't burble that he's hot or handsome. You can say you admire his professionalism, or his skill as a mechanic or his love for animals. He will get the idea that you like him but won't presume any shortcuts. Then if he doesn't follow through, you haven't lost face.

Should the admirer attempt a premature proposition, make it clear that you are not interested in casual sex. At. All.

You might mention that intercourse is not a proper expression between "friends" or between people who merely like each other. Sex is egregiously inappropriate outside of a loving, committed relationship. That was always true. It's still true.

Attract With Sympathetic Magic

To invite male energy into your life, increase the yang force in your environment.

Red sheets have been recommended to draw in a lover, along with a person-sized floor lamp by your bed. I don't recommend open flames anywhere but you can have glowing air fresheners or a red Christmas light that *looks* like a candle on your bed table .

It may help to put a photo of a herd bull up in your room. Not a snorting, rearing, dangerous, bull, but a nice, contented, fertile-looking bovine, standing in his pasture ready to service his cows. If you want to draw a black man into your life, you can download a picture of an Angus bull and paste it up. If you would like a white man, a Charolais bull would be appropriate. There are red bulls, brown ones, yellow ones, spotted ones...

7

Hey, do you like freckled men? If your dream lover looks like Conan O'Brien, you can put up a red, speckled, Beef Master.

Let The Stars Guide You

My sister, "Stella" (Not her real name. Her real name is Kate.) wondered why she had never been married or even had an enduring live-in relationship with a man. "Stella" had a pleasant personality and been beautiful in her youth so there was nothing drastically wrong with her. I looked at her horoscope and said, "You have Sagittarius, the bachelor sign, on your seventh house of partnerships. And you have no planets *in* your seventh house." I told her she would be surrounded by men if she went to live in the other end of the country. She chose Las Vegas as her favorite western city and moved there. Within a month, she began her first long-term live-in relationship with a man.

Two months later, she phoned to complain, "All the men I meet out here just want to go to bed with me."

I said, "Is that so bad at *sixty*?"

Ask your friendly astrologer to try your birth chart in different cities to favor the issue you're concerned with. You can relocate to improve one aspect of your life, but be aware that you would be giving up some good fortune you have been enjoying in another area. For example, your astrologer can send you to some part of the world where you would easily find a husband, but maybe you couldn't get a decent job. Or she can send you to some place where you would make more money but maybe would be living in uncomfortable quarters or would have no friends or leisure time.

On-Line Match-Making

Many websites purport to make it easy to meet your soul mate. But be advised the odds are atrociously against finding your prince on the internet.

You must first construct your own profile, using a photo

that presents you as intriguing without being too flattering. If you're slender, show your whole figure. If you're plump, focus on your face. Should looks not be your strong point, emphasize something else. You can show yourself in a long shot, standing in front of your beautiful house. Or sitting on the edge of your desk in your posh office, or leading your horse down a trail. If you don't own anything that photogenic, you might have a picture of yourself in an interesting setting. Interesting to men, that is. At a NASCAR race, getting an autograph from one of the drivers. Ringside at a wrestling match. Shouldering your rifle in a deer-hunting camp. Receiving a trophy on a golf course.

No written description, however detailed, can give a true picture. My sister Mary has even charged that the bio on my own website is misleading.

"Oh, no," I protested. "Every single thing I said is true. I *did* climb pyramids at Chichen Itza. I *did* lead a conga line of 4,200 people along the marina in Gijon, Spain. I *did* make a reading tour through Germany."

But, she averred, by telling only the highlights of my life, I gave the (false) impression that I was an adventurous and exciting person, when actually I spend most of my time just hanging around the house, reading and watching television, eating, and going to the bathroom.

Well, yeah. But even the most exciting men in town, our firefighters, spend most of *their* time just hanging around the station waiting for the alarm bell to ring. And, yes, reading and watching television, eating, and going to the bathroom. So you shouldn't scruple to present yourself in your most flattering light.

Don't spend more than a couple of weeks e-mailing your prospect back and forth. If you have time to construct a full-blown fantasy version of him, you will be too disappointed when you clap eyes on the original and see that he's thin and scrawny or fat and flabby.

Warning: Natives of third-world countries go on dating

websites pretending to be Americans or Brits who are just *working* in those countries. They put up photos of handsome men they find on modeling websites. Sometimes their fractured syntax gives them away but not always. They have various tricks to swindle you. They may send you a phony check and ask you to cash it and send them the money. By the time your bank informs you that the check was no good and your account is being debited, your money is in Nigeria. Another trick is "re-shipping". They send you merchandise bought with a stolen credit card and ask you to please re-ship it to Lagos. The police come after you for credit card fraud.

Further Warning: Do *not* Google an old lover from your school days and contact him "Just to check in" or "to see how he's doing" unless you are *both single*. No good can come of it. Some women have ruined perfectly mediocre marriages over an illusory "connection" with a long-discarded romantic partner. "I haven't seen Harry in years, but he knows me so well," she bleats.

Nuh uh, sister. He knows what you were back in college: slender, pretty, and pliant. You've added many layers since then, and pounds and wrinkles and aches and pains. And baggage: a career or children or both.

We are not emotional vacuums looking for someone vaguely plausible to connect with. So we don't have to settle for the least repulsive body in our orbit and convince ourselves that he's what we've always wanted by dwelling on his good qualities.

"It's so clever the way he can live without any kind of job." Not good enough!

It's necessary to select the right sort of partner from the beginning. The right sort being that adorable darling who will live to serve you.

Fortunately, that possibility isn't so far-fetched. Remember that the human male, like his blood brother, the beagle, needs the security of a firm but loving mistress. Nearly all heterosexual men are wont to utterly adore some woman. For a few dreamers, she must be no less glamorous than Charlize or Angelina but many of them will be happy to settle for you. The trick is to determine which ones and then to choose from among them.

NO BOOK, NO EXPERT, AND NO SURGERY CAN HELP YOU ATTRACT A MAN WHO ISN'T DISPOSED TO DIG YOU ALREADY.

Certainly, you haven't been apprized of this heartrending truth before and I'm sorry you had to read it here first. But women must stop deluding themselves that an eye-lift or a session at Pilates will drastically alter some man's perception of them. As you embark on your search for the ultimate, all-giving lover, you must arm yourself with some understanding of the male psyche.

Your own image of the ideal mate probably changes in character and appearance every time you fall in love. If your current "Mr. Wonderful" is short and bow-legged, you feel positive vibes for all like short, bow-legged specimens. Next week you may see a Colin Farrell film and decide that scrawny, unshaven idlers with brogues are all the rage. Your perception of the ideal has been short-circuited.

Now you're about to learn that men are just the opposite.

The male has an indelible image that was imprinted in his mind, probably in babyhood, of his perfect woman, and he will not be wooed away from it. In fact, a man who has the financial means tends to marry the same woman over and over again, in successively later editions.

His phantom Venus may be of any physical type, but a man is usually attracted to the kind of looks his mother *didn't* have. If dear Mumsy was flat-chested and hippy, his fantasy love may be busty and spindle-shanked. If Mom was a fat cow, his dream girl could be dangerously emaciated. This divergence is good for the species.

Before offering yourself as a love object to a man, it is most important to determine whether you qualify for that role in

11

his life, and it's not difficult. Simply thumb through some photos of his ex-wives, girl friends, and favorite movie stars. There should emerge a pattern of facial features, shape, coloring, etc... If you largely conform to it, you're in. If you don't fit the mold, sorry, it's no go, so just cut your losses and split. Resume your quest for the prospect who will snap for your own brand of beauty and sex appeal. Do not try to cheat on your type and make yourself over into another to please the man of the moment. If you have curves like Drew Barrymore's, you can't be Angelina Jolie. All that dieting would make you sick and miserable

And why bother, considering that Drew has no shortage of admirers? Also, there are enough naturally-skinny women around to satisfy the demand for them.

And even if you managed to marry a man despite not conforming to his ideal, it would be no victory. Because he would spend all his leisure time between the honeymoon and the final decree ogling and slurping at women who do. Rotten for the feminine ego. Don't berate yourself for not conforming to a particular man's type either. And above all, don't be afraid that perhaps you're not *anybody's* type. Every normal, pleasant woman is a suitable facsimile of some man's fantasy image.

Whether you weigh eighty pounds or five hundred, you will have suitors to choose among. But the number of those available for your personal use follows the principle of the bell curve. Medium-sized women will have a greater range of possibles than those at either extreme of the weight table. Don't be overly concerned about this, though. Even if your physiognomy is so peculiar that only one-tenth of one percent of the men in the world are attracted to it, that still represents more potential lovers than you would ever have time for even if you spent the next fifty years on your back.

Happily, you don't have to go actively hunting for those men who are drawn to your type. Just make it easy for them to spot you. Decide which sort of allure you offer naturally and make the most of it. Not all men want stick-thin girls with unnaturally large breasts. There are as many lovers of hips and thighs as there ever were, but those unfortunates don't get to pant after their favorite parts anymore because women have been brainwashed into being ashamed of their voluptuous lower regions. If you have been endowed by nature with generous hips, don't hide them under a full skirt and decline invitations to pool parties. Rather wear something clingy to show off the good stuff and sashay proudly.

And now that you've resolved to be what you are, throw away that inflatable bra. It's only going to capture the interest of men who like big bosoms, and they're the last thing you need if you're an A cup.

Stars Bright

A "groupie," sometimes called a "celebrity bopper," and by all manner of less gracious terms, is a pinhead who offers herself for the sexual gratification of famous men. The absurdity of this practice is obvious. The male celebrity believes that his fame alone entitles him to a female's humble services and he needn't do anything otherwise to earn them. So he is even more arrogant than other men. And he may have less money to spend, after taxes, expenses, and drug scores than your average New York pizza waiter. And don't let yourself fantasize that a famous man is a better lover than an unknown. You may see "Apollo Starburst" in a film or on a concert stage and imagine that he embodies everything artistic and sensual. Understand, though, that once you have seen him perform, you have already had the best of him. His witty repartee has been written for him. He has been presented in his most flattering setting with his meager assets displayed to supreme advantage and his flaws ingeniously camouflaged. But when you see this stunner up close, in a good light, without make-up, you will find that he is four inches shorter than you had assumed and manifestly older than his press agent will admit. He is also pale and mottled of complexion sans his Max Factor pancake and markedly shriveled. His hair is either dyed or glued on.

Without his contrivances and illusions, he is as ordinary as your own husband. And maybe twice as obnoxious.

If you have sex with a performer, you won't be his girlfriend. (He already has a girlfriend.) You won't even be his one-night stand. As soon as you finish gratifying him in his hotel room, he'll hint strongly that he wants you to leave. If you try to hang around, he'll throw your clothes out the door, and when you bend over to pick them up, he'll put his foot on your rear end and propel you into the hallway. So you can have the adventure of re-dressing in public and making your own way home.

A very young woman whose ego is not yet formed (who doesn't know soap from Shinola) has great dreams of marrying a "star". She fondly imagines becoming the queen of his entourage, basking in his glory, preening at his table while he holds court for only slightly dimmer celestial bodies. She would give up her yet-undeveloped identity and her entire future to become "Mrs. Him" and to carry proudly his ermine-trimmed coat.

What she doesn't realize is that this life choice would be emotionally stunting. Stars have a way of absorbing any glory that's around, not reflecting it. And "Apollo", far from making a girl feel more glamorous, would actually steal from her the attention she would normally receive just being her own stunning, delightful, self.

The celebrity's wife must orbit in his universe instead of creating one for herself and contribute to the support of his ego at the expense of her own. What's more, a selfish creep who is rich and famous won't do her any more good than a poor and obscure one.

So don't marry a star. Better to marry a man who will help *you* become a star.

If you are determined to meet some notables in spite of these dire warnings, it's not impossible. You can get in touch with near-greats by entering industries that cater to them: budget limousine service, landscaping, toupee styling, or maybe dog

14

grooming. Even better is to buy something he wants to sell. If his hobby is painting, woodwork, or breeding parrots, decide you can't live without his still life, breakfront, or cockatoo and proceed accordingly. This entree isn't likely to lead to wedding bells but you may get to meet your favorite which should be enough to satisfy your curiosity.

"I've slept with thousands of girls; please be one of them."
Martin Mull

CHAPTER TWO: BEWARE OF SEX ADDICTS

A few years ago, I was standing at the counter in a computer emporium, got up in my usual winter ensemble: mink jacket over a grubby, shapeless, jogging outfit. My hair was braided or something, just to keep it out of my face, and I had no make-up on. I looked awful.

Spotting a soigné, well-dressed, professional man in the next line, I thought, "There is exactly the kind of guy who wouldn't be interested in me."

But somehow the fashion plate struck up a conversation anyway, gave informed advice about my computer needs and very quickly was coming on to me, smiling, brushing my hair back from my face and making those other little flirtatious gestures.

As I pushed my new P.C. out to the parking lot, he asked, "What are you doing later?"

I was flattered by the attention but was married to Richard, then as now, and headed straight home. I gave my usual answer to that question.

"Oh, my husband and I have a quiet evening planned."

Then I drove off with my virtue intact but singing to myself. "Tra la la la la. – Seems like the old gal's still got it."

Only later did I realize that there was nothing especially fetching about little old me. I had simply encountered a common, garden-variety, sex addict.

("What're you doing later?" is the mating call of the sex addict.)

I had become enlightened by the film, *"Autofocus,"* a biography of the popular actor and secret satyr, Bob Crane. *"Auto-*

focus" exposed sex addiction as *"The Days Of Wine And Roses"* did alcoholism, for the sad, sick compulsion it is, and should be required viewing for all attractive women, young and old.

My message here is that a proposition from a sex addict is not a compliment. Not even if the rampant skirt-chaser is rich, famous, and handsome, or used to be handsome. He has no more personal feeling for a sex provider than you had for any individual piece of chocolate the last time you binged on a Whitman Sampler.

Most male sex addicts are also compulsive voyeurs who have a hidden video camera pointed at their bed so they can record your episode of poor judgment and share it with their friends.

They aren't good lovers either. Since the addict doesn't make any distinction between you and the last hundred women he's made it with, or the next hundred, he's not going to do anything special to keep you around. It isn't the sex itself he craves, but the conquest of a vast variety of partners.

A misguided admirer of John F. Kennedy, who had been seduced by the president on his office couch, described a very unsatisfying episode. She thought they were just getting started when he jumped off, dashed back to his desk, and resumed his paperwork .

Here Is A List Of Famous People Accused of Being Sex Addicts:

Marv Alpert

Warren Beatty

David Bowie

The Sultan of Brunei (Can afford to fly in flocks of models and beauty queens for his parties.)

Richard Dawson

Kirk Douglas

Michael Douglas

David Ducovny

Robert Evans

Colin Farrell
Ralph Fiennes
Harrison Ford
Woody Harrelson (Accused himself)
Hugh Hefner
Timothy Hutton
Dennis Hopper
Billy Idol
Mick Jagger
Don Johnson
Bill Maher
Jack Nicholson
Kenny Rogers
Charlie Sheen (Surprise!)
Paulie Shore
Gene Simmons of "KISS". (Has more videos than Block-
buster, featuring his conquests.)
Rod Stewart
Adam West
Tiger Woods

Sex addicts are fewer in number than most other kinds of
addicts but very easy to meet because they circulate so much. If
you want to go to bed with one of these guys, that would be
easy: just be the most attractive woman he has access to at any
given moment. But first make him put on two condoms and a
diving mask. He's probably riddled with communicable diseases.

It would be more sensible just to say you *have* gone to bed
with any or all of them. They wouldn't be able to contradict you
because they can't possibly remember all their five-minute encounters.

When a man is basically a loser, has a high sex drive and a
great craving for multiple partners, but nothing to offer a beautiful young woman, (He isn't Hugh Hefner or the Sultan of Brunei.) he has to settle for those ladies who aren't very much in

18

demand: a little too old, a little on the ugly side, lonely single women, or bored housewives. Perhaps his fellow sex addicts.

There may be as many sex addicts among women but we don't notice them as much because they tend to stay indoors and nobody is complaining about them.

These desperate souls have a way to discover each other on-line. Ordinary, non-famous addicts have dedicated websites where they post their pictures and the descriptions they *wished* fit them and invite all and sundry to "hook up".

I once went on a cross-country trip with an emaciated blond I'll call "Ashley." She had a date lined up for every stop along the way. I would fall into my hotel bed, exhausted, after a fourteen-hour day, and Ashley would be putting on her make-up and running out to have sex in a car with someone she had never met before.

On Saturday, she had *three* dates. The first was an overweight Latin guy in Bermuda shorts who had probably told his wife he was going out for cigarettes. I guess he met Ashley's standards; she went off with him. The second was a decrepit, red-eyed, sleaze, apparently too disgusting even for her.

"You claim you're only *forty*? I don't *think* so."

And she sent him back down the stairs alone. The third was a young and handsome graduate student. Lucky number three could have done a lot better than Ashley, but he wasn't looking for a relationship, just a quickie with someone he hadn't made it with yet and she would do.

Big cities have support groups for sex addicts. (Though that reads to me like an opportunity to discuss one's alcoholism with an open bottle of Scotch.) You might suppose that their headlong quest would end at such a meeting. Guy sex addict connects with gal sex addict and they marry and live happily, passionately, ever after. But, no. Their compulsion is for an infinite *variety* of partners.

"Even a fool, when he holdeth his peace, is counted wise: and he that shutteth his lips is esteemed a man of understanding." Proverbs 17:28

CHAPTER THREE: COURTSHIP

During the get-acquainted ritual, it's a good idea to dance with your prospect. Slip an arm around his waist and check out the avoirdupois. Is he squishy or well-toned? Casually place a hand on his knee. Is it bony? Many men look like Adonis in a fine-tailored suit, then strip down to reveal paunch, flabby midriffs, skinny legs, and flat behinds.

If a man won't take care of his body, maybe you don't want to take care of it either.

Look closely at his teeth. If the cutting edges aren't slightly translucent, they didn't originate in his mouth. And if you absolutely require a tall man, be sure this isn't just a short man *pretending* to be tall. His knees should be halfway between his feet and his pelvis. If they're higher up than that, he's wearing elevator shoes and maybe two pairs of socks.

Now discreetly check him for tattoos. Beware if the man has more than one. And run like a rabbit if he has even a single *amateur* tattoo. He probably got it in the slam.

Most of your own self-disclosures will be verbal, properly enough. But don't tell a man your life's story early in the relationship. Better still, never tell him. There is nothing you can reveal about yourself that would be as fascinating as refusing to reveal. Even if you're the illegitimate daughter of Marilyn Monroe and JFK, conceived in the White House swimming pool, you would be wise to let "Mr. Right" elicit the breathless secrets of your past in brief, enigmatic flashes over the years and decades to come.

On no account must you entertain him with the most shock-

20

ing episodes of your personal history. If you spent your junior year abroad working out of a window in Amsterdam, keep the sordid details to yourself. At least until your fortieth anniversary.

At the close of your first conversation, if the prospect knows volumes more about you than you about him, then you have been talking too much. As usual.

A common seducer's trick is to get you blathering non-stop in order to learn what kind of man you're looking for, and then to become that. He will present himself as a sensitive poet, reckless adventurer, child-loving house husband, or any other role called for until he gets what he wants from you. After that, he's more than likely to drop the act and you'll find yourself toweling off with Mr. Hyde.

On the other hand, if you have just sat through a narration of his entire career and he knows nothing more about you than your phone number and bra size, then he's a self-involved boor, just using you as a sounding board, or an unpaid shrink, to nod and smile while he indulges his ego.

In the event that you and your new friend get along like a house on fire, ask to see his drivers license and note the address. (The con artist will refuse to show it.) If Mr. Tonight is just a married man in from the suburbs to find himself an easy piece, he may have been giving you a phony name.

Now (always) caution is in order. Don't ever go to a man's apartment, or even get in his car, no matter how charming and gentle he seems. You can not presume to trust a new acquaintance unless he is vouched for by someone who knows you both very well. The "thrill of spontaneous conquest" isn't worth taking a chance with your hide.

If the handsome prospect is really worth cultivating, he'll keep while you check him out. You can get further acquainted in a quiet restaurant within walking distance. Or take a cab there.

A man may ask for your phone number which doesn't

mean he ever intends to dial it. In many cases just the procurement of a woman's number and the promise it represents is conquest enough. In order to squelch this game of "Get the digits," claim that your cell phone isn't working properly or that you're never home, and ask for *his* numbers, both at home and at work. If he has been lying about his job or marital status, the truth will out here. And if he has no intention of seeing you again, he may give you phony numbers, but he'll never know whether you tried them or threw them away. If you do try them, make the first call from a pay phone so your name won't come up on his caller ID.

After you have parted company, you can go home and Google him.

"Better to keep your mouth shut and be thought a fool than to open it and remove all doubt." Mark Twain

CHAPTER FOUR: TALKING TO A MAN

When a man gets nervous in an intimidating social situation, he tends to shut up like a clam, just giving out the occasional grunt to show he's still alive. But a woman in a similar circumstance is likely to cover her insecurity by chattering like a magpie. He looks like the strong, silent type. She looks like a shallow air-head.

Any woman, however clumsy or ignorant, can cover herself in most social milieus by the simple device of shutting her yap. While silent, she remains mysterious, deep and fascinating. While prattling away about her mean old boss or the price of pantyhose, she reveals herself as an intellectual pauper.

You can get through an entire first date with phrases like "Mmm, really?", and "My, goodness; you must be proud of that." He'll think you're brilliant.

One summer evening, at Jo-Ann's Bar in Chicago, an intriguing local named "Ed" spun me his colorful life's story. Seems he had enjoyed several adventurous careers in his time, including stunt driver and convict. How nice. But as fascinating as this guy was, he couldn't have offered me much in the long or the short term, being a generation older and occupying a humble station in life, so I declined his request for a date.

Ed became very chagrined. You see, while I thought we were merely having an interesting chat, he had been making a "pitch" and assumed his gripping narrative would get me into bed that very evening. So, for him, it was an hour wasted.

The most common, yet challenging, form of social intercourse is the conversation.

23

Woefully, you will have much difficulty using this means of communicating with the other gender. Because, while women characteristically engage in discussions, men prefer simple bragfests.

For example, here follows some female-type conversation:

ANN: Yes, I have two children. Susie is eight and Bobby is ten. They go to St. Dominic's

BEA: Do they? I've heard that St. Dominic's is an excellent school. What do you think of the faculty?

ANN: Well, at the last P.T.A. meeting, I was particularly impressed by...

And it continues in that tenor. Contrast that pleasant exchange with a testosterone-reeking *male* conversation.

ART: So, listen! There I was clearing eighty grand a year before I was even twenty-five. It's a real rat race, I'm tellin' ya.

BEN: Yeah, I know what you mean. I quarterbacked at Tulane for three years. The pressure, man.

ART: Sure, but I didn't have time for football if I wanted to make Law Review at Fordham. Yeah, they wanted me for the team, but...

Ad infinitum.

No doubt you have gathered that the men's macho talk was not an exchange of information but an aggressive exercise in one-upsmanship.

Decoding The Lies Of Dating

The liar doesn't always expect you to believe his lies, in fact will express great contempt if you do.

"Sure I told you that. But you *believed* it? Geez, you're stupid."

But he thinks you should reward him for the ingenuity of his prevarications and skill at delivering them.

Here is a translation guide for a few oft-used lines.

    1. He says: "I love you."

    He means: "I want to make you."

    2. He says: "I'm looking forward to settling down in

one of those historic houses in Faubourg St. John, just as soon as I find a woman who loves the finer things of life as I do."

He means: "I *really* want to make you."

3. He says: "We're on the same wavelength, you and I. I feel a psychic sense of communication that I've never had with anyone else. Do you feel the same?"

He means: "There's nothing I wouldn't say to get into your pants."

4. He says: "I wish I could take you to some fancy restaurant, but I'm a little short this week."

He means: "You're not worth more than a sandwich."

5. He says: "Do you think I'm just after sex? Why, I could go down to Lucky's Tavern right now and have any woman I want for the price of a drink."

He means: "But you're here and you're free."

6. He says: "I can't pick you up till after nine."

He means: "By that time, you will have eaten dinner and I won't have to spring for more than a couple of beers."

7. He says: "Why go out in the weather tonight? I can fix you a delicious dinner right here at my place."

He means: "Thawed meat, tough as linoleum, instant mashed potatoes and last week's bread and margarine."

8. He says: "You understand that I am unusually sensitive for a guy."

He means: "I cry at dog movies."

9. He says: "I work hard and I play hard."

He means: "When I'm not in the office, I'm drunk on my ass."

10. He says: "I want to *share* with you."

He means: "My penis."

11. He says: "Sure, I want you to meet my folks, but they're sort of uptight people and I'm waiting for the right moment to tell them about our relationship."

He means: "Do you think I introduce my mother to

every bimbo I lay?"

12. He says: "I won eight thousand at the race track, but then some scumbag picked my pocket."

He means: "I lost all my money at the race track."

13. He says: "Age is only a number."

He means: "I don't mind schtupping an old woman like you if she'll support me."

14. He says: "I'll see what I can do for you."

He means: "Nothing."

15. He says: "I have great respect for you. I know you can't be bought."

He means: "I expect to get you for nothing."

16. He says: "I don't think of it as a conquest."

He means: "Ha! Score one more for me!"

17. He says: "I'm a top-secret F.B.I. agent."

He means: I'm a pathological liar who has killed one wife already.

If a person shifts his eyes to his left, he's engaging the imaginative part is his brain. That is, lying.

If he uses phrases like, "To be honest with you," and "To tell you the truth," he's lying. If he shakes his head while denying something, he's lying. If he avoids contractions, as in, "I would not, could not, did not, murder Nicole," he's lying.

Some famous lies don't even call for interpretation:

"They're shipping me out tomorrow."

"I haven't slept with my wife in two years."

"I'll only put the head in."

When a date says, "I'll call you," he means, "I never want to see you again in my life." So you should pretend to take him literally and counter with, "But I won't be home!" Stand up. "I'll be running non-stop." Grab your purse. "But I really enjoyed talking to you. Have a great weekend!"

And sail out the door, trailing your silk and furs behind you.

When he asks, "Can I call you?" he may truly want to see

you again.

Keeping It Simple

Your date will ask many questions for which the best answer would be an unelaborated yes or no.

Questions to answer in the emphatic negative:

"Do you want to lick this?"

"Are you any good at fixing grilled cheese sandwiches?"

"Like to see what's in my pocket?"

(In an expensive restaurant) "Aren't you on a diet?"

"Want to join the 'mile-high club'?"

"Would you like to help me clean out my shed?"

"Could you make me a copy of your key?"

"Want to go 'Dutch'?"

"Let's do something really crazy tonight."

"You want to see something really swell?"

"Got any money on you?"

"I know I can't do anything for you, but how about going out with me until you find a guy who *can* do something for you?"

"Wouldn't you like some real, pure, *protein*?"

And, conversely, here are some questions you must always answer with a yes:

"Are those real?"

"You think I need a shave?"

"Would you prefer to go by cab?"

"Do you mind if we stop at my place first?"

"Are you having dessert?"

"May I pay for the sitter?"

"Do you really have to go home tonight?"

"You think you're too good for me?"

Defining Parameters

Even during a casual chat over coffee, your male companion may use any number of tricks to dominate the conversation and, through it, the relationship. If, on occasion, you offer a political opinion that clashes with his own, he is wont to respond with a bellowed "Bullsh*t!"

Your genteelly-bred predilection is to back off and think, "Really? My goodness, but it seemed so logical to me," letting him take over.

His arguments won't make any more sense than yours, but they will be expounded in a louder voice and with apparently absolute conviction. You will politely hear him out until the subject is exhausted without ever having a chance to make your own thoughts known.

Hours later, after you get home, you may experience a gnawing sense of anger and frustration.

Another masculine manipulation maneuver is to orate at yawnsome length on a topic, then when you venture your own viewpoint, he'll interrupt with, "Can I just say one thing?"

The implication is that you have been monopolizing the discussion, so you guiltily shut your trap and he's off again.

(If a man gives you equal time to state your ideas and even refers to them while putting forth his own, either you're stinking rich or he hasn't got you in the sack yet.)

But now that you know he is making a power play, you don't have to permit it. If he breaks in on you with the "Let me say one thing." ploy, answer simply, "You have already had your say. Now it's my turn." When he greets your sincere and well thought-out opinion with a cry of "Bullsh*t!," or some similarly contemptuous dismissal, you can reply quietly, "I'm sorry you feel that way." and end the dialogue with a queenly exit.

If you have diverging opinions on a subject, his will be more worthy of expression than yours, even if you spent the last ten years studying the field and wrote your dissertation on it.

"Now, I'll tell you what *I* think about this," and onward ever onward with his thoroughly pigheaded pronouncements.

It is a masculine inclination to usurp any verbal exchange, and he does this easily by introducing a topic about which you know nothing and care less. Then he proceeds to "enlighten" you on it.

He will hold forth on the inner workings of the automatic transmission, or the intricacy of the quarterback sneak play, until you are bored to madness. If you're nervy enough to declare that you would rather not hear this tedious lecture, he'll charge that you are thoroughly ignorant and determined to remain so despite all his selfless attempts to acquaint you with the really important concerns of mankind.

Should you introduce a subject *he* knows nothing about, the man will announce that it doesn't interest him in such emphatic terms that you will feel like a bubble-head for even bringing it up. The triteness of your theme is evident merely in the fact that a brilliant individual such as he never bothered to acquaint himself with the matter. So he dismisses it or changes the subject. Or he stares at you blankly until you bring the conversation back to something worth discussing. Like him.

If you persist with the topic after this, he will bury his face in the sports section and shut out the sound of your voice.

(Unlike you, he won't even *pretend* to be listening.)

Men don't know how to end a conversation, either. Some years ago, I ran into a one-time date in an airport. After a brief, "How are you doing" discussion, he waved off with "I'll call you! We'll have lunch!" I smiled back. "Sure."

Mind you, he wasn't going to call me and I didn't *want* him to call me. We had no practical use for each other. But he knew of no way to take leave other than with "I'll call you." There are more appropriate exit lines he should learn such as, "Have a great weekend!," "Kiss the dogs for me!," and "Glad I ran into you!"

Most important is to know what *not* to say to a man. First, you should not talk to him about other men, good or ill. Worst is to talk about *one* other man.

Don't tell your prospect how badly your ex-husband treated you. He may infer that you didn't deserve any better. Neither should you tell him how *well* some man treated you. He'll think "Why didn't you stay with *him*, then?"

No matter how impatient you are to make a good impression, or to present yourself as a fun person, you must always keep your language clean and classy.

Do not reveal your erotic foibles and aberrations unless you are writing pornography for money under an assumed name. And never discuss sex in any context with a man until you're just about to undress him. Even the most abstract allusion to this area of human relations will prompt a man to assume (or pretend to assume) that you're willing to advance from the theoretical to the practical.

You may feel safe talking about sex with Willie, the sweeper, because he's hardly more than a derelict, older than your grandfather, and homely as a toad. So he wouldn't dream that he has a chance to bed you, right? Wrong! Even old Willie will presume that he has a shot at you. Even if your only conversation has been about your passion for Brad Pitt.

Yes, the male ego is a wondrous thing.

Verbal Abuse

Most of us learn to deal with normal male posturing, but a man may try to dominate you with phrases like, "You'll do it because I said so," and "That's when you get in trouble: when you try to *think*." and "*Now* you're doing something intelligent." (When you have done what he wanted.)

Respond immediately to such blatant attempts to undermine your self-esteem. Assert that your good opinion of yourself is not predicated on his approval.

Some men will try to make you insecure by criticizing other women.

"Look at that skinny broad," he may say, pointing out a complete stranger who is minding her own business. "I wouldn't f**k her if she *paid* me." So you feel momentarily grateful that he's willing to f**k you without being paid.

"Yes, she is skinny," you mumble, enjoying a brief moment

30

of rapport with the guy because neither of you has any admiration for this poor, unknown, skinny woman.

So what's wrong with that?

Well, first of all, your date would probably f**k a gorilla with trench mouth.

Second, it's the woman's own business if she's skinny and she never solicited your opinion of her figure or your boyfriend's either, much less offered to pay him to climb on top of it.

But most offensive is Mr. Macho's implication that no woman has a right to exist unless he is sexually attracted to her. He doesn't insult only the women he's deriding but all of us, everywhere.

He not only doesn't like women; he doesn't want his *woman* to like women. Should you express admiration for a sister of great accomplishment, he will retort, "That pushy lesbo? Why I wouldn't..," He displays hostility toward women who have achieved success in any field. The underlying warning is that if you assert yourself and improve your situation in life, you can lose that most precious of God's gifts, him. That's true in a sense. When you become wealthy and prominent, you won't care any longer to deal with this ego-smasher. You'll be feeling too good about yourself.

Take this with you: when a man denigrates other women by calling them "broads" or "sluts", don't attempt to ally yourself with him and against them. He means you too.

Saying No

Dana Owens, ("Queen Latifah") said, "I never handled pressure from guys well. I hated when they'd beg and beg. I broke down once after being nagged to death, and I regretted it immediately."

This brings us to the problem of declining gracefully. Imagine that old Willie, or some equally unappetizing piece of lard and bone would like to couple with you. You want no part of him. (Certainly not *that* part.) Do not let him whine, wheedle or browbeat you into complying out of weariness or pity. You are not a publicly-supported charity. You should be able to conclude the matter with a genteel but succinct rejoinder.

"You're a dreamer."

"Don't take this personally, but I prefer *attractive* men."

"I'll go with you for fifty thousand dollars. For a hundred thousand, I'll pretend to *like* it."

Or that old standby, "Ycch!"

Then you might ask the petitioner what you said or did to give the impression that you wanted him. Insist upon an answer. Then promise to stop saying or doing whatever it was.

When the heavy proposition comes from a man in authority and you're afraid that such flippancy will get you fired, you can secretly tape his suggestions and play them back for your shop steward, your general manager, your commanding officer, the E.E.O.C., or the aggressor's wife.

A more tactful way to deal with a grabby boss is to square your shoulders and declare righteously that sexual congress is not a frivolous undertaking for you but rather a serious expression of a deep-felt, long-term commitment. If he wants a relationship with you, he must leave his family, divorce his wife, and furnish a home for the two of you. It must be all or nothing.

Of course, this argument loses considerable sway if you've been staggering into work, day after day, in all stages of dissolution to boast of the number, variety, and dimensions of your conquests.

But if you have managed to keep a discreet silence about your sex life, you'll be able to present yourself as so throbbing with violent but unrealized passion that any involvement with you would jeopardize his marriage and all he has worked for.

It might help to refer to *"Fatal Attraction"* as your favorite film, declaring that you identify with Glenn Close.

One more note on the subject of talking to a man: Try not to make fun of his penis.

"To keep a man's respect, always give him less than what he wants, no matter what he wants."
The Bitch's Almanac

CHAPTER FIVE: FIRST DATE

We will assume that your wit, charm, and intelligence have impressed a man so much that he is just pawing the earth to know you better. But here are some caveats. When a new suitor invites you to "go out", don't just accept unconditionally. "Out" for him may mean nothing more than four beers at Duffy's and a hot-sheet motel. So make him commit to the nature of the "outing" before agreeing to set aside an evening for him. Don't sell your time cheap.

If your suitor is under twenty-five, maybe a movie and a snack at Wendy's are all he can afford. Be reasonable. But a man old enough and successful enough to be considered husband material must bring more to the table. And to a better table.

Some years back, I met a talented professional man, I'll call "Beemer." I had admired his work before we met and he had admired mine and we had so many good aspects between us that I was sure we would have a marvelous affair. So when Beemer invited me for coffee, I was dumb enough to put aside my day's agenda, dress up in my loveliest peplum suit and picture hat, and hurry across town to meet him. I thought he would devote the occasion to apprising me of everything he had to offer as a lover. But all that happened was some strained small talk over a stale piece of crumb cake. A few days later, Beemer called asking to see me again.

I coyly mentioned that I enjoyed dinner theater, expecting him to respond with, "Great! I'll get us two tickets for the dinner theater this weekend." Instead he came back with, "Dinner theater!? Why don't we just meet for *coffee*?"

Then I realized I had been ripped off. While getting dressed and made-up and curling my hair and trundling across town had taken my whole afternoon, he had just walked over from his office on his break. And he had never intended to spring for a proper evening's entertainment but figured he could win my sexual favors with a series of dry snacks.

When you meet a man "for coffee" that is recognized as a "pre-date" or an *audition* for a date. You should not travel out of your way, or get dressed up for this non-occasion. Give it about twenty minutes and sail out. Then if he calls you to meet again, he should be ready to invest in a "real" date. Dinner and a show.

[TIP: How to get a man to watch a chick flick with you: Tell him the two lead actresses are actually lesbian lovers.]

My pal Stephanie described a similar bust of an evening: "This college professor called and said, 'Get dressed up. I'm taking you out to dinner'."

So Steph bedecked herself most elegantly in satin and bows, heels and pantyhose, for her professor. And he took her to a *pizza* place! Naturally, she never went out with him again.

"If he had just said, 'Put on your jeans; I'm taking you out for pizza,' that would have been fine. But he made me get all dressed up!"

It probably cost her more to dry-clean her dress than he had spent feeding her. If the tomato sauce didn't ruin it altogether.

I've been snookered too many times. I once accepted a date with a man who then drove me straight to a highway bar.

I stopped at the door. "But I don't *drink*."

"Well, we have some time, don't we?"

I should have put my foot down then and said, "You can order a drink at the restaurant," but I didn't. After enduring an hour of noise, a bottled (not even fountain) soft drink, and mingling with this yo-yo's friends, only then did I learn that the next stop he'd planned was to be *his* place. There wasn't even going to *be* a restaurant. I walked most of the way home.

Don't make my mistake or Stephanie's. You must not accept a date without ascertaining exactly what it's a date for. When a man spends *your time*, he must spend *his money* as well.

You can determine his agenda without sounding too cynical. When asked for a date, you can purr "Sure, that would be *fun. –* Where did you have in mind to go?"

If he mumbles that you can work it out later, he's thinking beer and motel. Gently insist on the itinerary so you can plan and dress appropriately.

Suppose, for example, that you have used up a Saturday making yourself stunning in curls and lace for a heavy date, anticipating candle light, violins, and lobster. And suppose your swain of the month comes to pick you up wearing paint-spattered jeans. You have long been aware that men contrive to avoid expensive restaurants by under dressing.

"Gee, I'd need a jacket and tie for The Persian Room? We'd better try Wendy's."

So you are prepared for this. You may have a list of expensive places with liberal dress codes. Or you may have gone down to Goodwill and bought three presentable-looking jackets in small, medium, and large sizes along with a few ties. You pull out an appropriate one (implying your brother left it around) and offer it to your date.

HIM: (Smugly) "I've already eaten."

YOU: (Struggling for patience) "Why have you 'already eaten' when you knew you were taking me out tonight?"

HIM: "I wasn't counting on dinner. I figured we could just have a drink somewhere then maybe pick up a hamburger and come back here."

YOU: (Ushering him out the door.) "No, thank you. I've already f**ked."

Why waste your evening and calorie allotment on fifth-rate fare?

Another cheap trick is to pick you up for your date late

35

enough so all the nice places are closed. The skinflint may even go through the charade of driving you all over town to the finest restaurants, pulling into each parking lot just as the lights are going off.

"Gosh, I wanted to take you to La Maison d'Argent, but Burger King is still open."

So arm yourself with a list of good restaurants that are open late.

(Incidentally, the same fellow who drags you to Pizza Hut will reserve a private room at Antoine's for his date with an heiress. He reckons Miss du Pont will take a lot of impressing.)

Don't accept a date for an hour that's too late to go anywhere nice. If "Mr. Wonderful" calls to say, sorry, but he'll be delayed at work till nine-thirty, tell him to make it for some other evening.

When an admirer asks, "What are you doing tonight?" he's not likely to follow with "I'd love to take you to dinner at Brennan's and the touring musical at the Saenger."

What he means is: "I'd love to take you back to my office where we could do it on the couch in the reception room." Or "In the car under the South Broad Overpass" or "Up against a tree in City Park."

So, to the question, "What are you doing tonight?" The appropriate response may be, "Why? Do you want to take me out?"

If he insinuates that he thought he would just "drop by," you must explain, tactfully, that "drop by" happens about the fifth date. And only if jewelry happens by the fourth.

A first date is usually the man's occasion. You go to his favorite spots, get shown off to his friends, sit through his kind of entertainment, and spend the evening listening to him sound off about how wonderful he is. But you must be assertive enough to make your own choice in the matter.

Let's suppose he calls you because he's stuck with an extra ticket to the Rangers' Game but you don't like hockey. (Is that hockey?)

Him: "Hey, would you like to go out Friday night?"

You: "That would be fun! Where did you have in mind to go?"

Him: "I got two tickets to the Rangers' game."

You: (Cordially) "I'm afraid that would be wasted on me. I don't like ball games."

Him: "It's a *puck* game!"

When your sports fan assures that he will tell you all the rules of play so you can enjoy the hell out of it, just say firmly, "Thank you for thinking of me. Maybe we'll see each other at some event we both enjoy." Bye bye and hang up.

Don't sit through some cold, smelly, loud, raucous, athletic competition in the hope that your date will reward you afterward with a cordon bleu dinner in a fine restaurant. He'll expect you to fill up on stadium hotdogs and beer. Then he'll spend the rest of the evening rehashing every play. He may even plan to celebrate by having sex with you.

"But I took you to the *game*."

If your suitor leaves the choice of itinerary up to you, say you love French restaurants. They're expensive, so you rarely eat in one unless someone else is paying, right? And if you can afford it yourself, it isn't good enough for you. You should suggest a movie or a show after dinner. Read your local entertainment listings and make notes of places to go, or you'll find yourself down at Dinty's Pub, beer in hand, hearing forty-five-year old Clancy Brothers tunes on a bad sound system.

When dressing for a first date, it's especially important to choose something comfortable. Consider that you may have to run or fight and must be prepared. New heels are contraindicated because they will probably hurt your feet as well as make you taller than your escort and you will be in rotten spirits all evening long. A new blouse may scratch your neck. A new sweater may give you a rash. New pants may be so tight that you have to unbutton them during dessert.

Also, bedecking yourself in brand new clothes fosters the

delusion that the evening should be a glamorous, cinematic, occasion and could be a letdown for that reason alone. So instead of wearing a new costume, choose an old favorite which probably looks better on you anyway.

Some men make dates the way deadbeats used to make airline reservations, intending to show up only if it meets their best convenience. Taking an option on a woman's time costs them nothing, so why not? You had better try the airlines' method of dealing with these. (No, I don't mean over-book.) When he makes a date for Friday night, ask him to call back Friday afternoon to confirm it. If you can't get a confirmation, don't bother to dress and put on makeup unless and until you see him coming down the walk.

Nothing is quite so demoralizing as to sit all got up in your sexiest outfit, jewelry, and war paint, waiting at your front window long past the designated hour for the "date" who never appears. And then, sadly, to wipe off the make-up which hadn't had a chance to wear off, wriggle out of the pantyhose, dismantle your "sexy look", and hoist your still-unwrinkled best dress back onto its padded hanger for a hopeful future occasion.

Back to the couch to wait for your date. Give him a reasonable twenty minutes over the time agreed upon. If there is no sign of your escort by then, you may take yourself out to a movie or to visit friends. If the no-show ever runs into you again and apologizes for not keeping the date, just blink and say, "Did we have a date? I'm sorry I missed it."

But *don't* give him another chance. Standing you up was not an honest oversight but a blatant show of meanness and bad character. And a big, red, warning sign.

If you're going to spend the rest of your life dealing with men, you must first learn which of them *not* to deal with.

Okay, so far. Let's say your date came by after all and now you're out with him. Even if you have developed a marvelous rapport with this find, don't ever go up to his apartment unless and until you are ready to have intercourse with him.

Any excuses he gives you for stopping there: "I want to

38

play you my Mingus albums,...feed my gerbil... change my shirt..." are not to be believed because however elaborate the pretext to decoy you up to his place, once you're in the door, he will assume you have come for sex. And if you are naive enough to take him at his word and walk into the trap, he'll either call you a tease or assault you as punishment for being so stupid.

Then the police and the rest of the world will chuckle at your tearful explanation that you only went up there to help him turn his comatose mother over in her bed and all of a sudden, he ripped your blouse off.

Just stepping into his apartment will be considered consent in advance to anything he wanted to do to you. Had he mutilated you with an ax and eaten the pieces, his defense attorney would charge that your accompanying him to the scene of the crime was "asking for it."

If your date must detour to his building "...first, just to pick up my credit cards. Come in and have a drink," you must smile sweetly and say you will wait for him in the car. Or the cab. If he claims he'll be inside too long to keep the cab, then smile even more sweetly, close the door in his face and take the cab home.

If the man is married, bunking with a dozen fellow illegals, or living with his mother, he may not have an apartment to work with so will make a try at getting inside yours.

"Oh, you write songs? I would *love* to come up and hear you sing them."

Forget it, sister. He doesn't really want to hear your songs unless you're Alicia Keyes. He doesn't want to see your macramé either. Or to meet your cat.

Don't let him near the place.

This trap-avoidance rule doesn't apply only to his apartment or yours. Also read "lover's lane," work shop, mountain cabin, boat house, sometimes even an employees' lounge or supply room. Just don't go to any non-public place with him unless you have a chaperone.

(And by "chaperone" I mean your father or your brother or even your Aunt Minnie. *Not* his friend "Snake" or that dizzy Lisa from the office who is likely to pass out drunk on the davenport and leave you to fight alone.)

If a man tries to get you for a Friday, he's probably got something better planned for himself for the Saturday. Maybe she's a "sure thing" and you're not. (I *hope* you're not.)

And don't ever go to bed with a man on the first date unless you really don't care whether or not there's a second. Even dogs of uncertain ancestry take time to get acquainted before mating. (Take more time, in fact, than the average Californian, but that's neither here nor there.)

"Women have sexual desire; men have sexual tension"
Florence King

CHAPTER SIX: DON'T BE SEDUCED

I was rather naive when I got into the mating game. For the first twenty years or so. When a suitor would say, "I want to go to bed with you," I would read that as, "I am hereby announcing my vigorous campaign to become your lover and will shower you with gifts and attention to earn your priceless treasure."

But what he actually meant was, "I said I want it, so how about putting out right now? In the stairwell."

When a man makes a pass at a woman, however crude, she may infer that he is attracted to her and wants a relationship. Why, surely all he needs is a gentle lesson in deportment.

"Well, Eugene, I don't think we have progressed to the point where such intimacy would be appropriate. (Since we only met forty-five minutes ago in this airport.) So let's start going out together and see what develops. I'm free for dinner Friday night."

Then she goes home and waits for Eugene to call and begin a proper courtship. But he never calls. She doesn't understand what happened to his ardor.

"Why, he was wildly attracted to me. He said so himself."

No, he wasn't interested in her. He was just taking a shot for an easy lay. It cost him nothing to try.

When a man wants to have sex, but his real girlfriend is out of town or angry with him, he may try to connect with you for a quickie. Of course he won't admit that he'd forgotten you even exist until this moment of craving.

In the old days, he would excuse himself with "I tried to call you a lot of times but you weren't home."

That doesn't compute any more in the era of cell phones

and voice mail. Neither does "I tried to call but your line was busy."

So he'll go with "I've been itching to call you, but the office just got crazy!" or some similar alibi.

You can pretend to believe his explanation if you choose, but you're still much too busy.

(I once had a Cajun waiter knock on the door of my single-girl bungalow in the middle of the night claiming that he hadn't called because he'd been in *jail*. I sent him away.)

In the struggling-feminist seventies it became fashionable ("liberating") to pretend we women have the same undifferentiated sex drive men have. But we didn't, don't, and won't.

Why do you think about him all the time, constantly, while he seems to forget about you most of the day and go on about his business? Because we're mentally different from them.

Both hemispheres of our brains are hooked together while the males' are in separate compartments. Mother Nature has a good reason for arranging it this way. A man has to be able to activate only the left half of his brain and concentrate totally on his work. If he's out hunting, but day-dreaming about his wife back at the cave, he'll be eaten by a bear.

A woman, on the other hand, has to have a divided consciousness, right and left halves. If she's ever totally concentrating on her work and forgets about her baby back at the cave, the *baby* will be eaten by a bear.

When a man's "sexual" half is activated, the practical side shuts down. That's why he thinks it's a good idea to do it in the water at a crowded beach, claiming that no one would notice.

Sex is external for a man and internal for a woman.

It's incumbent on them to try to impregnate as many women as possible. It's incumbent on us to make sure anyone who impregnates us will stay around to provide well for the progeny. So there will never be anything "equal" about that activity. Women get pregnant and men don't. Women get bloated, lose their figures, get morning sickness, go through phenomenally-painful labor, then get stuck with a new human being they have to feed, school, and maintain for at least the next eighteen years. Women also have more tender equipment and so are more vulnerable to sexually-transmitted diseases.

A man considers a sexual encounter to be no more than an isolated experience, like going to a movie, a mere diversion of the hour. It means nothing and changes nothing. When a man propositions you, he isn't offering to hold you sweetly in his arms all night, introduce you to his family the next day and spend the rest of his life protecting you from the cold world. He does not believe that the gift of your body confers any lasting obligation on him, nor will he feel any special bond with you afterward. More probably, he just wants to relieve himself momentarily, with your kind assistance, and he won't care if you turn into candy cane after that.

What your great-aunt Loretta used to tell you is true. "The man plays; the woman pays."

Women, the keepers of the womb, know that sexual intercourse is inappropriate outside of a loving, committed relationship. That was always true. It's still true.

When Not To

Him: "You and I have got to get together."

You: "And do what?"

Him: (Uneasy laugh. Lowers his voice suggestively.) "What do *you* like to do?"

You: "Shop for jewelry."

If "Him" accuses you of being "materialistic", explain patiently that we live on a material plane.

By the way, when a man says he doesn't want a "material" relationship, that doesn't mean he's looking for a *spiritual* one. He still expects to enjoy all the pleasures of the flesh with you, but at no monetary cost.

Warning: Easy sex is not a short cut to intimacy because a man won't feel any closer to you after the act than before. Actually, he's more likely to put further distance between you.

Anything that easy to get isn't worth having, he thinks.

And don't ever put out "on spec."

Do not ever go to bed with a man as a favor to him. You would regret this act of charity soon enough when you realize that he doesn't half appreciate the "favor" much less repay it. You could puff and grind yourself dry throughout the whole Craig Ferguson Show, catering to his most disgusting perversions. (Your date's, not Ferguson's.) And at the end of the ordeal, his attitude will be that you enjoyed it just as much as he did and he owes you nothing.

Should you believe something important can happen with a candidate, a long-term affair or marriage, let your relationship build gradually. If he is really interested in you, you won't lose him by saying, "Let's wait."

A man who won't wait before sex won't wait around afterward either. He's strictly for the poke and run.

You should consider early sex only when your date is gorgeous and magnetic but otherwise inadequate. Not a keeper.

But let us assume now that you have taken a liking to your prospect and after a thorough investigation can trust him enough to be alone with him. Where to go? Your place or his?

His place, no question. Partly because your boyfriend is a lot less likely to behave badly if it's his own neighbors who will hear the noise and not yours. And if he gets too aggressive, you can send his bowling ball through his TV screen to punctuate the word "No."

Also, here is an opportunity to learn about the man. If "Mr. Right" has been lying to you about his wealth, marital status, or living arrangements, the truth is to be found here. (Realizing this, he may claim that his home is unavailable because his parents are visiting from Ellenburg. Do not accept any such excuse.)

But the main reason to choose his apartment is that, if he bores you to tears, it's easier to leave his place than to throw him out of yours.

Now, suppose it's your fourth date, your handsome escort

has spent a fortune on dinner and a Broadway musical, and you have just imparted the happy news that you will accompany him to his home. He is justifiably elated. But beware again. If he stops at an all-night market to purchase cucumbers or kielbasa, do *not* proceed to his apartment.

No detours. Very well, here you are at his place. You have already searched all the rooms for children's toys, checked the closets for feminine attire, and are satisfied that he is unencumbered. Now it's time to start the end of the evening.

Do not undress in front of a mirror that's set into the wall without first going around to the other side to determine that it's not a one-way window with a camera behind it, loaded and running. (One test of a mirror is to put your finger tip against it. If there is a space between your finger and its reflection, this is a righteous mirror. If your finger seems to be touching its reflection, it's a spy job. "If there's no space, leave the place.")

Also, make sure there are no microphones, video recorders, or even cell phones in the room. Check the light fixtures.

If your gracious host isn't visibly aroused by the time you've got your clothes off, pull them back on and call a cab. For, if the sight of your naked pulchritude isn't enough to turn him on, sister, he isn't really attracted to you. In which case, what are you doing there? Or he's got problems which you are neither paid to nor equipped to deal with.

Should you experience a saintly calling to rehabilitate the sexually handicapped, go work for a clinic as a sexual surrogate and you can make some good money at it. In any case, don't waste any time trying to arouse Mr. Limp-As-A-Sweatsock. You could be back home with a good book.

But let's imagine instead that all goes well. Your admirer turns out to look great in his skivvies, he can hold his breath a phenomenal length of time, and makes you blissfully happy.

Once recovered from these hedonistic love rites, put your clothes back on immediately, even if you have a shape like Miss December and whether or not you intend to remain for a postcoital chat. Most men don't want to look at a naked woman right after sex any more than they want to stare at leftovers after a full meal.

Also, sitting around in your pelt makes you look available and a man never appreciates what he doesn't have to work for. Even if you want seconds, dressing again apprizes your lover that he has to take the time to woo you all over again.

Never spend the whole night, after your first encounter. To sleep over on a one-night stand is both tawdry and pathetic, giving the impression that you haven't a decent place of your own and would sleep with anyone just to get out of the wind. (Your first heavy date must always be considered a one-night stand unless and until he calls you again.) The man who most pitiably begs you to spend the night with his lonely self will be the least happy to discover you there in the morning.

When a drunk whimpers, "I need you to stay with me tonight," it doesn't mean that he needs *you*. He simply feels that he needs *someone* warm to sleep with that night. Then when he wakes up the next morning, sober and hung-over, he'll react as though he's just found a smelly old stray mongrel in his bed.

"I hate to rush you out of here, but I've got an early meeting."

Or, "My ex-wife is coming over with papers for me to sign and I can't let her find you here."

Or, "I promised my son I'd take him fishing this morning, so... I'll call you."

No breakfast, no nothing.

Also, it's no treat to meet the grey dawn in an unfamiliar apartment, far from your own toothbrush and fresh underwear, with a bleary-eyed, stranger.

Another consideration is that your partner will probably wake up in a tumescent state. And if he finds you in bed beside him, he'll think he has the right to pass it to you, even if that's the last thing you feel like doing. So you either endure his unpleasant attentions or fight him off while grabbing your clothes and making a half-naked exit via the fire escape.

Then it's left to find your way home, to shower, feed the dog, change clothes and try to grab a bagel on the way to work so you won't faint from hunger.

Is this any way to start the day?

So it's vital to your comfort, as well as a strategic move, to leave your lover's place in the dead of night. But do not allow him to give you cab fare. If you accept his paltry twenty dollar bill, he's "sending you home in a cab." If you pay for it yourself, you're "leaving in a cab". There's a world of difference.

Though if he orders you a limousine on his account, it's okay to take it.

Should your first tryst take place at your own apartment (against my best advice) don't ever go off to work and leave the man there as he's liable to steal something. (I once had such an overnight guest "borrow" my favorite jeans and I never got them back. The dinner he had bought me wasn't worth the cost of the jeans.) Should the man dawdle around while you're dressing, exhort him to snap it up. If he asks to stay "another few minutes for another cup of coffee", tell him you can have a cup together downtown. Say your mother/daughter/landlady is due to drop in and she mustn't find him there. Say whatever you have to but don't budge from the place until he is safely out the door. And it and all the windows are carefully double-checked and locked behind him.

It's better to be late for work than to return home to find your wine cabinet looted.

CHAPTER SEVEN: EN GARDE

Conducting a romance is akin to the sport of fencing in that it calls for a strategy of advance and retreat. The difference is that, in romance, the retreat is the power play and the advance the concession.

You must advance when you want your prospect to know you're interested, then retreat and let him come after you. Advance when he's feeling depressed, insecure, or unloved. Retreat when he tries to dominate you or takes you for granted. And when he withdraws from you, that's when you *really* retreat. Leave the field altogether.

You would lose a great psychological advantage if you see your date as a potential partner, therefore an ally, while he sees you as a potential conquest, therefore an adversary. There you are both fighting for the enemy and no one is fighting for you. (Except your mother. Always listen to your mother.)

A common cad's tactic is to begin your association with a big rush: constant attention, phone calls at work, avowals of great admiration and empathy, allusions to marriage and skyscraper erections. You get the whole Valentine's Day scene with red hearts and fat, little cupids. But then as soon as you appear to return his feigned affection and his battle is won, he'll turn about and distance himself. Emotionally, if not geographically.

You can use a gentler version of the same tactic. When you meet a desirable man, throw yourself at him with great enthusiasm. Then when he, flattered and flustered, leaps to take advantage of his serendipitous conquest, you back off and tactfully lay down your ground rules. Just make it clear that even though you find him attractive, you will not allow him to treat you with less than tenderness and respect. And generosity.

This is not a tease. After all, you *are* willing to fulfill the man's wildest and most voluptuous carnal desires, but on your own terms, not his.

(Be sure to deliver these conditions early enough. Don't wait till he's got his *thing* out, for pity's sake.)

You already have him imagining himself in bed with you. Now he suggests that you adjourn to his room. Or to a car. Or behind a tree, or wherever. This is when you quietly inform him that you are not available for a fling. There has to be a serious relationship between you before you get physical.

YOU: "I'm not interested in casual sex at all."

HIM: "Oh, no. Me neither. – It wouldn't be casual."

YOU: "Great. Then what kind of relationship did you have in mind for us?"

HIM: "Uh, well... What do you want?"

YOU: "I enjoy being good to a man and I require that he be good to me too."

HIM: (warily) "How do you mean 'be good to you?"

YOU: (Demurely) "First of all, I don't want you to buy me expensive presents if you can't afford them."

HIM: "Don't worry about that."

YOU: "Don't worry?"

Now you must get a clarification. If your suitor assures you that you shouldn't worry because he can afford plenty of expensive presents, things look promising. But should he indicate a lack of funds or disposition to be generous, then don't order dessert. Just cut the evening as short as possible without actually making a scene. There's no point in wasting any more of your time or his money when you can be home watching "House" with your cat.

Until he has made great strides toward meeting your needs, you must not be led into a compromising position. That is, don't be alone with him in any place where intercourse would be possible: in a car on a lightly-traveled road, an airplane with automatic pilot, a walk-in closet, etc.

You probably can't use sex to manipulate a man if you aren't giving him any at all. But always give him less than he wants. If he's going for three times a day, make it once or twice. If he likes it every day, make it four times a week. Not only will the scarcity keep his appetite up, but if you're ready any time he is, he may feel insecure. Like maybe you're ready even when he *isn't*. And if he gets the idea that you enjoy it as much as he does, he'll start thinking he's doing you a kindness. Then you will never be able to use your favors as bargaining chips.

It's time to be practical in your choice of consort.

The oft-touted attributes like intelligence, wit, wealth, and position are all to be desired. But burn this into your mind: no matter how many sterling qualities your partner may have, he is absolutely useless if he does *not love* you.

Your treatment at the hands of a man who doesn't love you will be pernicious and degrading. The brilliant one will use his intelligence to make you feel inferior. The rich one will spend his money elsewhere. The well-connected one will think too little of you to introduce you to his connections. So whatever qualities you think a man should possess, love for your precious self must come first.

A power play at which men are adept is the meaningless apology buttressed by the "puppy-dog bit". This technique allows a man to conduct himself in a most reprehensible manner in the confidence that all will be easily forgiven.

The "puppy-dog bit" involves getting really cuddly. Your man may coo baby-talk while laying his head in your lap and whining that he couldn't help doing what he did. He's just a baby, after all, and it's up to you, the mommy, to love and understand him.

The meaningless apology is often accompanied by a very sentimental but otherwise totally inadequate gesture: a box of candy for standing you up for the concert of the year, a frilly new night gown for a black eye, or a romantic dinner out for leaving you broke and pregnant in Eunice, Louisiana.

Some men have discovered that they can be as inconsiderate, even as brutal as they like, so long as they intersperse episodes of rotten behavior with brief periods of the puppy dog bit. The only way to keep him in line is to insure that each trespass guarantees him a hardship at least twice as intense as the pleasure it afforded him.

Do not identify with your lover. His motives and concerns are not the same as your own, and in most aspects, will oppose them.

Don't believe anything he says.

Never trust a man who asks you to trust him.

Always get the money first.

"I don't mind if a man loves me and leaves me, so long as he leaves me enough." Anonymous

CHAPTER EIGHT: MEN AND MONEY

A penis is more valuable than a college degree in the U.S. job market. On average, a woman earns only seventy-six cents for every dollar a man makes

And "liberation" or not, men will continue to enjoy this advantage for many years to come. (Until we take over.) So bring this to mind the next time you get some stupid idea about paying your own way on a date.

At that golden moment in the distant future when women have the same opportunities as men and equal power and equal money and we see as many skirts on the Senate floor as trousers, you may feel honor-bound to kick in your share of an evening's expenses. Until then, nothing is equal. So don't be a jerk.

Watch Out For Cheapskates

Some years ago, I had dinner in New York with a fellow writer named Herb.

"As long as I've been married, I have never spent one penny on another woman," he avowed. "Not one *penny*."

I was relieved to hear that he had no romantic intentions toward me. (In those days, men seldom sought my acquaintance unless they hoped to get me into bed. The main disadvantage of being young and rather pretty.) For there was no surer way for a man to avert an affair with me than to announce that he had nothing to offer. On our second or third meeting, I was appalled to learn that Herb actually dreamed that I might go to bed with him some day. For nothing! The old tub (and he was old) was a sex addict before the term was invented.

A man like Herb believes it's all right to cheat on his wife several times a week, so long as he treats the other woman badly. "She was just a whore. She meant nothing to me."

To emphasize his contempt, he would be stingy with his mistresses, giving them nothing but a lot of self-congratulatory chatter and his short, fat, bald body. I had to advise him that if he leaves his money at home, he should stay home *with* it.

(At least he paid for the dinner. I wouldn't have sat and listened to him if he hadn't.)

By the way, when a man suggests going to a restaurant, you must ascertain whether he's "inviting" you as his guest, or merely "proposing" that you join him and pay your own way.

You can determine this tactfully, by asking, "Do they take credit cards?"

The only acceptable answer is, "What do *you* care? *I'm* treating."

If he says anything else, you have to rush home and feed your dog.

Some men will spend a million words to save one penny. A suitor may call to say, "You're the most intriguing woman I've ever known. I've been thinking about you all day. I wish I could take you out for dinner; but I'm short of cash, right now."

He hopes you will respond with, "That's okay, you charmer. *I'll* pay for the dinner."

But what you will actually say is, "Some other time then, when you're more flush. – Oops! I've got to run and feed my dog. Bye, for now."

If the caller is just looking for a mark, he'll take the hint and move on.

A few years back, I was attending a conference in Seattle, walking through the lobby to the bar, when I ran into an acquaintance from New York. He waylaid me there, just outside the bar, for a long chat about the publishing business and friends we had in common. When he had exhausted me of conversation, he ended the encounter with a cheery "Catch you later" and sashayed into the bar by himself. Then I realized that he had kept me from entering because if we'd had our chat inside, he would have been expected to buy me a drink.

If you walk into a bar alone, you may spot a man you know who won't even turn to acknowledge your presence until you have ordered and paid for your own drink. Then he will recognize you all of a sudden, greet you with great fanfare and be chatty and affable until you get down to the ice, at which time he'll spot someone across the room whom he's been dying to meet for months and lurch away.

Cheap men often try to masquerade as generous ones. For example, I knew a sales manager who would take his crew out to lunch and make a big show of picking up the check. He impressed the restaurant staff as generous and prosperous. But once he got outside, he would collect from everyone. So this won't happen to you, be sure to get the scoop from the moment you sit down. Ask loud enough for the server to hear. "Are you treating? Because I didn't bring much money."

Another tactic is for a date to give you a sum of money which you would assume is a gift, say to pay your rent or reimburse you for groceries, and for which you would show suitable gratitude. But then he would gradually bleed it all back from you.

"Now, are you going to take me out to dinner?" or "Look, I gave you all my money; so can you charge a pair of trousers for me?"

It wouldn't be long before he has mooched back all of his "gift" and more.

If a man hands you money, you should ask right out: "Is this for me?"

If he says "Yes," then thank him effusively and run and put it in your bank account immediately. If the bank isn't open, use it to pay your rent ahead or spend it right away on clothes, groceries or other necessities.

Some stingy men think they can earn a place in your life by being great lovers. The problem there is that if they don't spend a modicum of money they won't get a chance to prove their

54

skills as lovers.

Me, I don't care if a man is good in bed so long as he's good in Tiffany's.

"If virtue is its own reward, why not a little something extra for being bad?"
An ad for Fortunoff Jewelers, featuring Lauren Bacall.

CHAPTER NINE: PRESENTATION

Flowers and candy and such are lovely gestures but they don't count as presents. Neither does dinner out. Nothing you can't re-sell is a present.

Apparel or paraphernalia accommodating his fetishes are not presents either. You don't need crotchless underpants or velvet handcuffs.

When you desire a token of esteem from your admirer, first make sure he can afford it. If he can buy you the gift, still meet his rent payment, and have enough left over for bread and soup, then he can afford it.

(And if you make him pay dearly for every minute of your company, he will all the sooner want to marry you, if only because the courtship is breaking him.)

Of course it is necessary to extract a present from a man *before* going to bed with him. Once he is sated, his outlook will be less generous.

Or to put it more crassly, once he's had it, he won't think it's worth anything.

Never whine or wheedle for a gift. Such would be demeaning. Simply mention that you would like a such and such. If he says no or maybe later or anything but "Let me buy it for you," just smile good-naturedly and go home. Refuse further dates with him.

Expect presents of clothes and money as your due, and if your rich boyfriend hesitates to unzip his wallet, unload him right away before you get too attached to the tightwad and start thinking that you love him for himself alone.

My friend Zelda was dating a physician and she made it clear (she thought) that what she wanted for Christmas was a diamond tennis bracelet. When that festive day arrived, the distinguished man of medicine presented her with...a *teddy* bear. Zelda figured then that her diamond bracelet must be *inside* the teddy bear and tore the toy apart looking for it. No nothing. She found another date for New Year's.

If a man tries to pass off a child's toy as a gift suitable for a grown woman, don't coo and giggle and act girlishly grateful. Just say, "How cute. My six year old neighbor would like this."

(But I would keep the teddy bear if it came with an emerald collar.)

A tightwad may even be low enough to break up with you just before Christmas or your birthday so he won't have to buy you a present. He may then attempt to resume the affair again after the occasion has safely passed.

Make-up presents should be twice as expensive as those for other events.

There is a type of man who proposes to a woman, gives her an expensive engagement ring, enjoys her gratitude and affection, then ends the relationship and demands the ring back as a "gift given in contemplation of marriage". So the "fiancée" was simply ripped off for all that gratitude and affection. The ring will be cleaned, re-sized and passed on to another sucker.

Simply don't give it back. Should he take you to court over it, your argument will be that the ring was not given "in anticipation of marriage" at all because his intentions were never of the honorable variety. He was just leading you on with false promises.

You may be able to prove the man never really planned to marry you: If no date was set. If he had just signed a long lease on his bachelor apartment or made other plans for the distant future that didn't include you. If he didn't tell his friends or family about an upcoming marriage.

If either party was already married at the time of the "gift" then it can't be "in contemplation of marriage".

The laws regarding engagement rings vary from state to state. In some states, if a man calls off the marriage due to no fault of the woman, she may keep the ring.

If you live in a jurisdiction where you would be required to return the ring, it would be *wrong* to swap out the stone for a cheaper one. So whatever you do, do *not* go to a jeweler and have that done. Certainly not using your own name.

When your boyfriend offers you an expensive gift, ask for a piece of jewelry other than a ring and accept it on some occasion such as Valentine's Day or your birthday. He can also write you a note such as "For the anniversary of our first kiss" so it's clearly not an engagement present which he can demand back.

There is a recognized art to getting clothes out of a date before he gets you out of *your* clothes. One tested ploy is to invite an admirer to go shopping with you.

"I want to buy a dress *you* like, darling."

Drag him to a fairly swank store and let him sit while you "model" fashions for him. Tell him the prices and if he declines to like any of those dresses, haul out some more expensive ones. Then offer to take him to fancier shop. When he finally indicates the frock he dislikes least, trot him over to the cashier. If he doesn't pull out his wallet, you must pay for the dress yourself. (You can exchange it tomorrow.) Never stop smiling and bubbling. After all, he doesn't owe you a dress. And you don't owe him your delightful companionship either. Part company as soon as you hit the sidewalk. The association was unproductive.

If your man of the hour buys you an expensive gift with a check, don't "thank" him for it until the check has cleared, the bank assures you that the funds have been collected, and the item is officially yours.

Go shopping early in the day so the store can call his bank and confirm his account balance.

The plethora of mail-order catalogues makes it easy for the

greenest amateur to score some nice cadeaux. Invite your light o' life into your living room, sit him down with a drink and maybe loosen a shoulder strap so he starts salivating for delights to come. Then get out your favorite catalogue and cuddle up to him.

"Isn't this an adorable necklace, Poopsie-pie? I was hoping you would like it enough to buy it for me."

What can Poopsie-pie do now? He'll probably say, "Sure, hon." in which case you leap up ecstatically, give him a hug and a kiss and ask for his credit card. Call the twenty-four-hour, toll-free line and place your order. Then you must let him tell the operator his credit card number and explain he's sending the item as a gift so they will have his voice on record and no one can say you stole his card number. Then specify overnight express delivery and close and hide the catalogue so he can't call right back to cancel the order.

Naturally, if he says no to the request, you will get a terrible headache and show him the door.

It has been rumored that some men get a lot of mileage out of a single expensive vendible by giving it to one woman, enjoying her "gratitude," then taking it back and bestowing it on another. Should a man present you with, say, a fur coat, ask him to write you a card "as a wonderful memento of the occasion."

A little note like: "Dearest Dot, this mink will keep you warm while I'm away, Your Jim." will be an indication of his intent and your lawful possession. Next best is to get your admirer to state that it's a gift, not just lent for the evening, in front of witnesses. One could be the waiter at your favorite restaurant.

"Mr. Forbush just gave me this coat. Isn't he a doll?"

Once he has given you a present, don't let him get his hands on it again. Not to have it glazed or taken in or anything. Sleep in it if you have to. Or put your bicycle cable through the sleeve and padlock it to your plumbing fixtures until you can have your closet reinforced and fitted with a combination lock.

Get it insured as soon as possible and have the skins under the lining indelibly marked with your driver's license number.

If your swain offers to fly you to St. Moritz for the skiing or to Tokyo for the kabuki, be sure to get your round-trip ticket from him in advance, in your own name and non-transferable. Also get enough travelers' checks for emergencies. It wouldn't do to strand yourself penniless in some exotic locale where you don't know enough of the language even to hustle yourself a meal.

Take a course in gemology and buy yourself a jeweler's loup. Learn to evaluate all gifts on the spot. If a man tries to win you over with zircons, or Nigerian "Swiss" watches, reward him with a folded slab of raw liver. Fake jewelry rates a fake vagina.

Cash should always be welcome. But when your admirer makes you a gift of money, don't waste any of it buying something for him. He won't really appreciate it and will probably be discouraged from giving you any more money.

Don't think you should help a man save for his future, either. Face it, sister: there is very little chance that future will include you. The only assurance you would have of that would be his handing his paychecks over to you. In this rare and wonderful event, husband the money as carefully as you would your own, socking it into the bank, stocks, money market funds or real estate depending on the financial climate. All in your own name.

(If you decide to dump him, you must give at least half the money back. It's only fair. But he will think awfully hard before dumping *you*.)

If an admirer "gives" you a car, don't be too grateful too soon. His intention may just be to let you drive it for a while. And then he can even sue you if you damage it. Don't so much as mumble a thank you until you've got the title in your hot little fist, duly transferred by a notary.

TIP: Keep a friendly notary on speed-dial, one available day and night. Then a con man can't put off making a legal transfer.

Don't be cheered if a suitor recites incidents of outrageous generosity to his wife or children. His magnanimity may de-activate at the inside of his front door.

Milking the Cream

On your first meeting with a successful man, he just might spend the evening bragging about the multi-million dollar business he built up from nothing, his employees, cars, boat, plane, etc.

Unfortunately, though, he doesn't intend to spend any of this great wealth on *you*. Well-heeled males think they're owed the unlimited services of beautiful women just because they *have* money and they needn't *spend* any of it.

On your first date, "Gotrocks" may presume that just hearing about his acquisitions will send you into paroxysms of passion and lay you at his disposal.

The next time you encounter such a blowhard, you can put him away appropriately.

HIM: "...So there are lots of rewards to running your own Fortune 500 corporation. I mean, I can buy anything I want, you know? But there's a lot of pressure, too. Say, it's time you told me about yourself."

YOU: "I'm a real maniac in bed. Can't help it. I just love to kiss a guy all over, run my tongue around his fipple, do the hot water trick, the bead trick, the ice cube number,... I can go on like that all night. And I have a snapper that drives them wild!"

HIM: (Gulping down his drink.) "Great! Let's go to your place."

YOU: (Wide-eyed.) *My* place? Why whatever for?"

HIM: "To get it on. All that good sex you're talkin' about."

YOU: "Oh, dearie me. I wouldn't dream of it."

HIM: (Red-faced now.) "Then why were you sayin' all that stuff about what a hot piece you are if you weren't gonna give me any?"

YOU: (Innocently) "Goodness. You've been going on all evening about how rich you are, but you haven't given me a car or a diamond watch or anything. I thought it was supposed to be all *talk* tonight."

Finding yourself a big-hearted sugar-daddy is not as easy as the romance novels would have you believe. There are many more beautiful and greedy ladies than rich and generous men, so you must study tactics first.

The commonest delusion of a gently-bred woman is the belief that she must be modest and unselfish with a rich admirer. If she never asks Moneybags for anything (she reasons) but quietly and submissively flatters his ego and serves his every whim, perhaps he will reward her devotion with a nice present. Like a condominium.

Women have been using this approach with wealthy men since the dawn of civilization. *And it has never worked! Not ever!*

Men don't value anything that comes to them without cost or effort. Our hypothetical pampered rich guy will only presume that you get your jollies doing the slave number and he's showing you a kindness by allowing you to fawn all over him. He may even aver that his *time* is so valuable that you're lucky he's "giving you" *that*.

(If your beau spends the day doing your taxes or cleaning out your cellar, he is indeed "giving you his time". But when he merely whiles away the hours enjoying himself in your company, it is *you* who are giving the time. It depends upon whose agenda is being addressed.)

Don't mistake a man's extravagant self-indulgence for a sign of generosity, either. The same guy who happily pays five dollars for a glass of water (carbonated, with lime) is likely to presume that a strenuous night of recreation with a beautiful and charming woman should cost him nothing.

When taking up with a new admirer, it's vital to institute a pattern of heavy spending from the beginning.

First be honest with him and with yourself. Admit right away that what interests you is his power and savvy about finance. Do *not* pretend that you would love him just the same if he were the night counterman in a Lebanese diner. Why let him kid himself that he has acquired some irresistible magnetism all of a sudden?

A wealthy man may try to keep all his wealth for himself with talk of "cash flow problems." Of course, he would *like* to give you everything you deserve but had to borrow thirty thousand on a short-term loan to meet payroll this month, there's been a slow turnover of inventory, and his biggest client is late with his payment for the quarter.

So you figure you must do your part by fixing casseroles and having your dates in front of the television until things get better. Like a sucker.

If you will look closely, you will note that Mr. Entrepreneur isn't depriving *himself* of anything during these lean times. He hasn't sold his Porsche or moved to a smaller billet. The cyclical ups and downs of his business have no effect on his lifestyle or personal spending.

YOU: "Poor Milton. I'm sorry you're having business reverses and I certainly don't want to be a drain on your finances. We'll just suspend our relationship until you're in a better position."

Blood From A Stone Dept.

You should not concern yourself with saving your escort's money. If he doesn't spend it on you tonight, he'll only waste it on himself tomorrow. Or on some other woman. So go ahead and make the best use of it while it's at your disposal. If you modestly suggest McDonald's when he can afford Antoine's, he will not appreciate your thrift. And he certainly won't reward you for it by buying you a new dress with the money saved. Furthermore, once you've offered yourself as a low-cost companion, the man will balk at spending serious money on you.

And never go Dutch on a date. Not ever.

If your admirer is too cheap or too improvident to spring for your movie ticket, see the new Drew Barrymore film with your friend, Susan, or the gay guy from downstairs. The conversation will be better.

Do not let a man take up your time on the phone either. He could waste the best part of your evening whining about his problems while you assure him that he's a wonderful person. You're being ripped off. He has most of the benefit of your company for no more than the cost of a local phone call, while you would rather be watching the hunks on "Smallville." If he wants to talk to you about his troubles or the wonderment that is himself, he can do so over a lobster dinner at Galatoire's. That's a bargain compared to the $3.95 a minute he would have to pay for professional company on the phone.

It is up to you to decide what your time and attention are worth, and then not to settle for less from the man who covets them.

(We know you've been taught "It's a sin to sell yourself." But that's much preferable to giving yourself away for nothing.)

On the other hand, your escort may put on a big show to impress, stopping in the most expensive nightclubs, ordering fine wines, dropping a fortune in tips, etc. then expect you to fall over backward. "I just spent five hundred clams showing you a good time."

What he really did was show *himself* a good time and the company of an attractive woman made his display all the more ego-gratifying.

Make it clear that if he had wanted to spend that money on you, he would have let you order a nice little silk number from the Saks catalogue.

It's possible that you cast your beady eye on some gorgeous younger guy with blond curls and dimples. Even the admirer with no money can contribute to your welfare in some tangible way by doing your yard work, wallpapering your kitchen, painting your portrait, or the like.

"Exactly what kind of 'love-making' do you expect to accomplish with me sitting in this chair, fully-dressed, and you standing in front of me with your dork hanging out?"

Disillusioned Date

CHAPTER TEN:
HOW TO PLEASE A MAN SEXUALLY

The message of this chapter is *Don't bother!*

So there is a new man in your life. (Let's call him... um... Dick!) Before you invite him into your bed, he will think you untamed, mysterious, and enchanting. But once you have given him what he's out after, you'll be degraded to "used goods", mundane and soiled. Do not sell your initial advantage cheap.

And right about now, you're squealing "Ooh! But I'm so good in bed that he'll just *love* it and be mine forever!"

Nertz, sister.

Let's just suppose that you knock yourself out giving "Dick" the best time he's ever had. You can draw on every chapter of the Kama Sutra, throwing in suggestions from Penthouse Forum and bits of business from "*Eyes Wide Shut*" and he'll be impressed all right. But he'll be more inspired to share you with his bowling buddies than to marry you.

No normal adult male ever fell in love with a woman just because she was skillful in bed. If she is of the particular physical type that turns him on, she can just lie there like a halibut and he'll be thrilled with her anyhow. If, on the other hand, she doesn't fit his ideal of feminine pulchritude, the poor cow can toil over his supine and smirking form until she gags and it will gain her nothing of value. Sure, he'll enjoy these attentions well enough but he won't *love* her for them or reciprocate in any tangible way.

At the outset of an affair, the spirit of conquest and your mere unfamiliarity as a sex partner may keep "Dick" in a state of arousal. But once the novelty has faded, he may hint that he needs additional stimulation. He may vocalize his should-be-secret fantasies during the act itself, ("Oh, Britney! You're mine at last!") and so ruin your chances of enjoying it. He may even try to make you participate in his quirk. Perhaps he can only get excited by hearing you describe your dalliances, real or imagined, with the neighborhood delivery boy.

("Hey, baby! Tell me how you made it with that pizza guy! Was he big? Huh?")

Or he may lapse into baby talk, call you "Nursie," and outline a scenario in which you play some fanciful dominatrix role, thus turning what should be a mutually-pleasant episode into a tedious chore for you.

Or he may eschew proper intercourse altogether preferring that you watch in rapt fascination while he abuses himself raw.

Do not lend yourself to these practices. Be aware that if you give in to some repulsive and disgusting demand just once, you will find yourself stuck in that role forever.

If your suitor expects you to furnish such services, hand him the Yellow Pages and advise him to look under "Escort Agencies." He can find a nice lady who caters to such aberrant whims for a living and gets paid very well. If you're going to bed with this clown for free, your primary motive should be your own quest for pleasure. You are not there solely for his.

Some males would describe as "good in bed" any woman who is willing to gratify them to the utmost in that manner (You know the manner I mean.) which affords no satisfaction for herself. The man who demands this kind of interaction is so indifferent to women that he doesn't want the involvement of coitus. He prefers to lie back and inhale a cigarette while his partner serves him as something between a slave and an appliance.

Don't *ever* gratify a man in this way unless he reciprocates. First!

But if he isn't willing and eager to attend to *you* in that manner, it bespeaks an unhealthy revulsion for the female body. And he'll be the "taker" rather than the "giver" in other areas of your relationship too. Don't go back for seconds.

Many a man doesn't even make a sincere attempt to please you. What he really wants is for you to please *him* while squealing that you're having the time of your life in the effort. But don't ever fake enjoyment just to flatter his ego; you would be working against your own interests. Instead, tell your lover exactly what you want the very first time. Then should he refuse your modest request ("I don't go that route.") don't pretend that you're perfectly content with his technique anyway. Worse is to think you must "prove your femininity" by seeming to pop all over the place under the clumsiest of attentions.

Express your dissatisfaction by expressing *him*. Out into the street!

Do not postpone enlightening your lover while allowing him to fumble along indefinitely. Because then when you finally do apprize him of your needs, he'll realize that he had been doing it wrong from the beginning and will then bristle, square his shoulders, and declare that nobody's ever complained before and there must be something the matter with *you*.

Tell him what turns you on physically but don't reveal your private erotic fantasies. Not ever. If he finds out that you have to imagine Hugh Jackman naked on a bicycle to find your way, his colossal ego won't be able to deal with it. So just tell the guy you were thinking about *him*.

Yeah, he'll believe it.

Here are a few additional tips about dealing with male sexuality:

1. If you leave it alone, it will go down by itself.

2. In case you care, his most sensitive area is in the cleft of the glands.

3. Urinate immediately before and after intercourse to forestall cystitis.

4. Most men don't like it when you make too much noise.

It's distracting.

5. Don't ever let anyone handcuff you.

6. Never give the most precious gift of your body to a man who is too drunk to take his own shoes off. Believe me; it won't be worth it.

7. The "backache" is the uninterested man's functional equivalent of the woman's "headache".

8. Semen is an emetic.

9. Unless your man is built like a gherkin, don't let him push your legs up over your head and have at you like a band of pillaging huns. The battering ram approach can result in bladder irritation, infection, and even fractured ribs.

10. Should your date protest that the very nearness of you has excited him to such a level that he can't contain his passion, advise that he be excused to the men's room where he may relieve himself in a toilet stall.

(Ignore his irate claim that he would never resort to this manner of self-gratification. HE DOES IT ALL THE TIME.)

11. If it doesn't feel good, don't do it!

Some X-Rated Observations About Men's Things.

If he has an enormous member, he won't be able to keep it up long enough to do you any good. A man who is generously endowed doesn't know anything about foreplay either. He figures that just unrolling it should be enough to make you quiver with passion. Going in dry, it will be full-sized, and hard and painful. But by the time you get lubricated enough to enjoy it, it will go soft which is very frustrating, like trying to have sex with a wet rope. And it won't get hard again until two seconds before he finishes. Then he will declare that you must have had a glorious time; so lucky were you to experience the wonderment that is his thing.

Men with really small things have had to learn everything about foreplay to compensate. So they can get you all excited, but then they don't have anything of note to stick in there. So you're still frustrated. Best is a man with a medium-size thing that can be counted on to stay up.

A dollar bill is six and one-eighth inches long, good to know if you ever want to measure his thing without being so crass as to use a ruler.

Why a man is better than an electric vibrator:
1. No distracting buzzing sound.
2. The rigidity/flexibility can be optimum.
3. Naturally contoured for an exact fit.
4. Responds to verbal commands: "Slow down,... Faster,... Longer strokes, ..." etc., so both hands are free for other business.
5. Doesn't need cords, batteries, or preheating.
6. Can be used underwater.

"Like a diamond, Herpes Simplex II is forever." The Bitch's Almanac

Unsociable Diseases

A most frightening indication of heedless promiscuity is the growing epidemic of venereal disease. Gonorrhea is an example of a disease that men are aware of shortly after contact. (Their urine burns and they are well, well aware.) While women may not know they've been infected until the damage is irreversible.

Conclusion: You may transmit the disease to a man without realizing it. But if he infects you, it's with full knowledge of what he's doing.

Some years ago, a millionaire socialite was successfully sued by a woman whom he had infected with gonorrhea on a weekend fling and rendered barren.

A young lover of Rock Hudson's successfully sued Hudson's estate because the star had sex with him and failed to mention that he had AIDS.

We can hope that such lawsuits proliferate and force the

general run of males to be responsible for their actions.

But while waiting for men to develop a social conscience, you had better learn what every prostitute knows about protection from disease, a measure termed the "short arm inspection."

Short-Arm Inspection

Before getting intimate with a man, keep the lights full on for a thorough inspection of his private parts. If there is any sign of sores or lesions, active or dried up, they indicate highly-contagious Herpes, and I suggest you call your date everything but a voter and get the hell out of there.

If the skin is clear and unblemished, you're not home free yet. Grasp the gentleman's schlong firmly under the glans like a gear shift, then squeeze hard, pushing down toward the base. If any pus comes out, this man has been preparing to infect you with gonorrhea. Let him know how you feel about that.

(You must not allow your new intime to urinate before you check him out as this would wash away the evidence.)

Then look for genital warts which are also contagious and may indicate Human Papilloma Virus, (HPV), which causes cervical cancer. Now part the pubic hair to examine for body lice. Body lice look like little crabs, but you don't have to know that. If you see *any*thing scurrying around in there, you should end the evening.

The religious application of this survey will cut down your chances of catching something nasty. But there is no fool-proof protection from all the many venereal diseases in all their myriad stages of contagion. Other diseases, which you can't see, are HIV, Chlamydia, and hepatitis.

Never operate without a condom until you're at least engaged and both of you have been tested for every sexually-transmitted pathogen known.

Your purpose in using the condoms is as they used to say on the box, "For prevention of disease only."

A venereal disease specialist of local renown has observed that a person who has been drinking heavily is more liable to become infected than a sober one. It could be that alcohol reduces one's resistance. Or that one who is intoxicated feels less pain so pushes harder and acquires sores and abrasions for germs to enter.

Another factor is that the drunk is considerably less choosy about whom she goes home with and doesn't look very closely once there.

Some Final Points:

1. Herpes is contagious *before* the outbreaks. Sores still invisible on the lips can be transmitted to the genitals or even to the eyes where they can cause blindness.

2. If a man tells you he has a venereal disease, don't reward him for his honesty by going to bed with him.

3. Never go to bed with anyone you don't know well enough to sue.

"The ideal man has only one weakness: me." The Bitch's Almanac

CHAPTER ELEVEN: SORTING THEM OUT

The new man in your life should be more than a jar opener that eats. What does he have to offer? Companionship? Do you really need his companionship or do you already have plenty of friends who would make fewer demands on your time and energy?

Most males have about forty-seven minutes of interesting conversation to dispense and after that, it's just ranting and raving. If he drinks, it's *slurred* ranting and raving.

Mind you, if he is full of charm and delight and you're some unpleasant old trout whom no one wants to be around, then, yes, you're lucky to have his company.

Sex? Well, if all you want is sex, you can get a younger, better-looking man.

Is your relationship paying for itself as it goes along? If it ended tomorrow, would you be grateful for the time you spent together and all he gave you, or would you feel ripped off?

"Why, I put up with his garbage all this time because I thought he would: marry me..., teach me to fly his Cessna..., put me in his band...."

So get out a pencil and paper and figure up exactly what benefits you have been reaping from these squalid entanglements. What good things have you taken away with you? If last year's Lochinvar gave you three hundred shares of a no-load fund, count this a concrete benefit of the association. Also, if he tutored you for your bar exam or taught you jujitsu, be glad you met him.

What else might you have got out of a relationship? Don't write "Great sex" on your list of positives. That factor is ephemeral and subjective. "Great sex" is of no lasting value unless this worthy gave you your first orgasm, in which case, you may light a votive candle for him every anniversary.

If he took you out to fabulous restaurants, that doesn't matter either once the food has been digested. But if, at the same time, he taught you how to order wine without sounding like Larry, the Cable Guy, mark the plus column.

If he flew you to Rio for the carnival, another plus. Travel is broadening. But if he flew you to Rio *and* sprang for a desperately-needed overhaul at Doc Pitanguey's, even better.

The most portable of acquisitions are money and learning. Take all of the former you can get, of course. The latter, though, is of no benefit unless you will find it useful later. Learning to tune a car engine is educational. Learning to please Fahrquar by dressing up in leather and barking Nazi commands is merely degenerating.

Write down what you have acquired from each of your men in terms of service, material wealth, and knowledge. Then divide it by the amount of time you spent with them. If Ralphie gave you a mink coat during a two-month whirlwind fling, you did great. But if you slogged around after this joker for three long years for the same coat, you came out far behind.

Don't discount the depreciation from aging. What have you got to show for those years of wear and tear on your body, mind, and heart? Darned little? Sorry.

So smarten up. Before getting involved with yet another man, stop to consider what he can do for you. Will he *enrich* your life or merely *complicate* it?

When you fall in love, you are giving custody of your happiness over to someone else. And any momentary thrills you experience in his company may be more than offset by the long hours or days of aching frustration and craving you feel while away from him. So can he bring you something special enough to compensate for all you will lose in time and tranquillity?

If all he has to offer is dinner in a nice restaurant, is it

73

worth your time to get dressed up in something that has to be dry-cleaned and be sweet and charming all evening, and maybe face a wrestling match at the end of it? Can you really enjoy your filet mignon if you have to listen to his yammering about himself and the orang-outangs he has to deal with at the office and how a poor sap like him can't catch a break due to a universal conspiracy, the whole evening? Maybe you would rather be home watching a Lifetime movie in your pajamas and eating your own cooking.

If you stay at home and *knit* every night, in a couple of weeks you will have a very nice sweater. If you keep some boring man company every night, in a couple of weeks, you will only have let your laundry pile up.

Before you take on a new consort, make it clear in your mind what you want him for. Women traditionally have expected to find the qualities of a sexy, fascinating, lover and a sweet, reliable, husband all wrapped up together in the same man. Members of the opposing sex, by contrast, have always known this to be improbable and, historically, they have chosen their wives for fertility, chastity, and industry and their mistresses for personality, sophistication, and erotic allure.

It's long past time for the distaff side to realize that husbands and lovers are two different breeds, each to be sought and evaluated on its own merits.

Here are some factors to judge by:

Age:

A lover should be much older than you (that you may profit from his wisdom and status) or considerably younger. (That you may absorb some of his energy and refresh your viewpoint.)

A husband should be about your own age, so you can keep up with each other, you will be growing older at about the same rate and have the same peer group values.

Solvency:

A lover should be rich if you're poor and poor if you're rich.

Your husband should be in the same socioeconomic bracket. Inequality of class and income would carry over into other areas of the union.

Background:

A lover should be from some exotic locale or milieu. This divergence will give you something to talk about between sessions and you can broaden your knowledge of other lands and their peoples.

A husband should be of a similar background so you will have the same reference points and won't despise your respective in-laws.

Financial Disbursements:

A lover should be a compulsive spender, flaunting his wealth by arraying you in fine clothes and jewelry and taking you to the best places. He can be a high roller who takes you to Vegas on weekends and gets all kinds of comps from the hotels. Once he has gambled away his stake, of course, you have to move on before he starts asking you for loans. Don't let him take you down with him.

A husband should be frugal, content with a wardrobe assembled from garage sales and bent on investing every dollar at maximum return.

Physiognomy:

A lover's looks aren't important. If he turns you on, you'll get a charge out of him, moles, cavern chest, bald head, pot belly, or whatever. Besides, you will be meeting him in distant motels and dark alleys so no one important will see what a gargoyle you've taken up with.

But a husband is a different matter. You will be looking at his gob, for better or for worse, season in and season out, from now on, introducing him to friends, and having pictures taken at family gatherings. Well, you don't want to have to *apologize* for the guy. Also, ugly men beget ugly children.

Marital Status

Hey, sister. *I* don't care if you fool around with a married man. You might be in some country where that's considered perfectly all right, like France or some place, but be sure you are forewarned of his status.

If a man gets you into bed by representing himself as single, free to love you and get involved and all, and subsequently you learn that he's married, then call his wife and tell her what happened and offer to testify at the divorce hearing.

I would.

For a quick roll behind the back bar at Lucky's, it doesn't matter whether your partner is married or not. But a long term association with some else's husband is a sucker deal unless he's paying for your car, your apartment, and your law school tuition.

Only a prize fool would give it away free to a man who is supporting another woman. You're doing her work for her while she enjoys the benefits. You might as well show up at her house next Monday morning and give it an attic-to-cellar spring cleaning for nothing.

And never feel you owe it to a married man to be faithful.

Choose Younger

Brigitte Bardot said, "For every year a woman grows older, her lover should be a year younger."

Ivana Trump said, "I'd rather be a babysitter than a nurse."

Women usually seek out lovers who are older, smarter, and more sophisticated than they but this may be short-sighted.

The man who has the advantage of age, more education and status will become the de facto principal of the union from the outset. He may patronize, usurp and condescend while the less experienced woman fails to develop any strength or ego of her own. She gives up her personal identity and defers to his tyranny until that inevitable day when he tells her she's become a bore and walks out. The futility of this trend is easily read in the listless and disillusioned faces of your verbally-battered girl friends.

Advantages of robbing the cradle, or at least the campus,

are obvious. The young man is prettier and lasts longer. He has the strength and endurance to provide sex on demand. Your demand. No need to feed this boy oysters or to parade around in a thong. He seems to have swallowed a steel rod and is ready at all times. Also, he's flexible enough to learn and carry out your favorite techniques.

"Just keep moving your tongue up and down on that. I'll tell you when to stop."

Certainly your best lover will be the one you train yourself.

When a man loves a younger woman for her youth and innocence, it follows that he must love her less with each passing year. But if he loves an older woman for her wisdom and sophistication, he should love her *more* every year.

Glancing about, you may notice long-term unions between sophisticated women and their younger, less-seasoned lovers. As the senior member of the party, leadership will fall to the lady, uncontested. Leadership is enriching and strengthening in many ways. Accept it and enjoy it.

Choose Dumber

Choose dumber on *purpose* that is. Many a woman has taken up with some anemic, four-eyed, nerd under the illusion that he's brilliant. But once he has exhausted his introductory line of pedantry, he is revealed to be a one-subject idiot savant who thinks Plutarch is Mickey Mouse's dog.

To avoid this crushing disappointment in advance, you might scratch "brains" off your list of requisite masculine qualities. You're not likely to find them anyway. Having proper awe of your superior intelligence, the simple man won't try to out-argue you and will defer to you on all the important decisions. And, most practically, you can take charge of the household finances. Yes, it's tedious to fill out the income tax forms and handle the checking account, but for this little effort, you will gain control of all the funds. You will budget the money prudently, knowing the optimum amount to allocate for clothes, hair salons, and presents for the lifeguard at the club. You will also be building a substantial savings account (in your own name) in case of emergency. And you could be sending generous gifts of cash off to your mother in preparation for that sad day when you and your sweetheart part company.

But, referring to the previous chapter, don't make the mistake of *marrying* the younger man. Every picture of Ashton and Demi should carry the disclaimer: "The Kutchers are movie stars. Their case is not typical. Your results will vary."

Choose Innocent

The man who loves a more experienced woman has already transcended the antiquated double standard of sexual mores. He can't even pretend to believe that males have license to visit countless bedrooms while women must remain chaste. He knows you are as capable of foraging as he and this alone should keep him in line.

Choose Straight

The company of homosexuals is like junk food, spicy and delicious but not really substantial. Naturally, gays are more fun than straight men. They have a sense of style, advise you on clothes and hairdos, keep you company till dawn, and share their liquor with you. But the homosexual isn't going to give you his paychecks or mow your lawn when you're old and feeble.

Gay men are delightful escorts and companions but they fall short of their hetero counterparts in some regards. For those very factors that make men useful to us are by-blows of the infamous male posturing that nellie types aren't burdened with. Male generosity ("check-grabosis") is a manifestation of this.

Hetero Joe boasts of his earning power by spending money where people can see it, i.e. spending it on you.

Reckless bravado is another outgrowth of the male ego. When some foul-mouthed drunk hurls threats and insults at you across a barroom, Joe may go punch him out, even if he's ridiculously over-matched. It makes you feel special to have your honor defended, however inappropriately.

Regarding sexual performance too, the straight man will be a better partner. He may be more crude and less imaginative but he is also less discerning. Just the sight of your radiant nudity should arouse him on the instant so he won't stop to analyze the sag of your breasts or your inventory of cellulite. He also has a longer attention span.

Unless your gay friends are directly helping you with your career (which they may do if you're a fashion editor or an interior designer, for example.) limit your social engagements with them to once a week or fewer. Mainly because a flock of Tinkerbelles fluttering around your place will scare off the straight men who are your real prospects. They may conclude that you can't function in a normal male-female relationship. Or, worse, that you don't know the difference.

By the way, it's not difficult to sort men out by sexual orientation. Around about six-thirty in the evening when the straight man really seems to need a shower, the gay man will look like he's just had one.

Falling Hard

The "grand passion" is as intoxicating as any drug and can turn a sweltering afternoon in a seedy motel room into a thrilling intrigue. But, like any other drug, it also carries undesirable side-effects. It can be-fog the mind, unsettle the excretory system, and, at its lowest point, cause the user to become dangerously depressed. Even suicidal.

Being in love is like checking into an opium den. It seems like glorious fun while you're in the midst of it, but once you have run through all your money and got tossed out on the curb, you realize that you hadn't accomplished a blessed thing while you were "blissed out" in there.

A compulsive romantic tends to "chain smoke" men. That is, she can't stub out an old love affair until she's got a new one started.

Or, as the Spanish say: "One nail drives out another."

If you keep meeting the same exploitive man under different names, if your life is a constant round of falling in love, with its euphoric highs, and breaking up, with its suicidal lows, you may have a chemical imbalance. Ask your doctor if you should take MAO inhibitors to allow increased output of your own phenylethylamine and to regulate your wild mood swings.

Many unhappy women don't have a series of affairs but rather experience the same affair over and over with a series of men. This mode of conduct is about as edifying as sitting through Prof. Sludnik's "History Of The Cumquat" course for twenty-seven consecutive semesters. And always pulling a D.

And even the memories are too revolting to be enjoyed now that your head is clear.

There are swarms of wretched females who think life isn't really worth the effort unless they're constantly tossing about in the throes of a great romance. No single mortal, however attractive, can evoke such passion interminably. This feeling, like any drug, wears off in time, necessitating a fresh dose to achieve a new high. So the miserable fool will discard a perfectly good partner when the excitement wanes, and go hunting for a new one to rekindle the thrill and the magic. Not necessarily a better man. Seldom a better man. But just a breathing slab of meat to hang her fantasies on.

Nobody is immune. Beauty doesn't confer immunity. Marilyn Monroe was rejected by men she wanted to marry. Neither does wealth. The richest young woman of her day, Christina Onassis, had to bribe her own husband just to spend the night with her. And she had to put up with his slender, blond, and beautiful mistress who had a baby by him around the same time Christina did.

Here follows a list of rich, famous, and beautiful women whom you and I can feel superior to because they were much stupider about men than we are:

Edie Adams: Her big-spending husband, Ernie Kovacs, was

killed in a reckless driving accident and left her two stepchildren and enormous debts. Miss Adams worked like a mule for years to pay off all the creditors and raise the stepchildren.

Clare Bloom: When she married the (rich, rich) novelist, Phillip Roth, she signed a pre-nup relinquishing any rights to his assets. She spent all those years abjectly serving him and ended up with nothing for her efforts.

Doris Day: After her husband and "business manager", Marty Melcher, died, she learned that he had gambled away her entire fortune and she had to start all over in her mid-forties. No longer a bankable movie star, she was forced to take a vapid TV sit-com to put food on the table.

Jane Fonda: Let her first husband, Roger Vadim, gamble away her inheritance and bring other women into their marital bed. Let her second husband, Tom Hayden, spend her fitness-video fortune on his causes and political career while she lived in a crummy shack to please him. Then after sixteen years of marriage, he dumped her for a younger woman. Her third: whacked-up, egomaniac, Ted Turner, was her *good* ex-husband.

Anne Hathaway: The young and beautiful film star dated the supposedly-rich Italian business man, Raffaello Follieri, for four years, before it came out that he was nothing but a con artist who was embezzling millions from trusting investors.

Rita Hayworth: Orson Welles got her to cut and bleach her beautiful hair, put her in a film that failed at the box office and left her a million and a half in debt. (That was like twenty million now.) All the while, he was cheating on her. And he was her *good* ex-husband.

Katharine Hepburn: devoted the best years of her life to a cranky, self-absorbed, drunk (Spencer Tracy) who wouldn't divorce his wife to marry her.

Paris Hilton: unwitting star of a sex video.

Lauren Hutton: Spent her sixty-million-dollar fortune financing trips and fulfilling the dreams of the man she loved. Even though he married someone else during their relationship.

Ali McGraw: Miss McGraw was the most sought-after young brunette in Hollywood when she married Steve McQueen. He demanded that she, A: stop making films to become his full-time wife, and B: sign a pre-nup relinquishing any claim to his assets and income. When they split up six years later, due to his womanizing, he got the money, the house, the furniture, the pots and pans, and she got her jeans and t-shirts. By then she was nearly forty and her stardom a dim ember.

Debbie Reynolds: When she married the shoe magnate, Harry Karl, he was a millionaire. But then he gambled away all of his own money and all of Debbie's and left her deep in debt.

Diana, Princess of Wales: The most glamorous, photographed, and admired beauty of all time fell for a married art dealer and "stalked" him on the phone, calling dozens of times a day. She would also park her car down the street from his house and sit in it, hoping to catch a glimpse of him coming or going. Then she fell for an irresponsible playboy who got her killed when he ordered his drunken chauffeur to outrun some photographers at any cost.

Esther Williams: Supported her first husband, Leonard Kovner, through medical school while he cheated on her with a nurse. He demanded all her savings as the cost of a divorce. While Miss Williams was working fourteen-hour days at MGM, her drunken, unemployed, second husband, Ben Gage, disposed of her real estate investments behind her back and gambled away all the money. Her third husband, Fernando Lamas, demanded that she give up her stardom to stay home and cook and clean and wait on him hand-and-foot, which she did for twenty-two years until he died.

The Predatory Male

Pablo Picasso said, "For me there are only two kinds of women: goddesses and doormats."

Some men don't think of women as worthwhile and feeling human beings, but as trophies or sexual appliances. And for them, deceiving a woman is not a moral trespass but merely a legitimate means to a worthy end.

HIM: "We'd better cool it now, Elizabeth. You've been getting too serious."

YOU: (bewildered) "But, Dougie! *You're* the one who made it serious. You said you loved me and were considering marriage."

HIM: "I had to tell you what you wanted to hear."

Of course this justification has more holes than a rock star's left arm. You did *not* want to hear that he loved you if it wasn't true. If he was only saying it to break down your resistance and make you vulnerable to his exploitation.

If a man finds it easy to say, "I love you," he's doubtless had years of practice.

The predator will lie about his age, occupation, income, marital status, number of natural teeth or zodiac sign, adopting any fiction appropriate to conquer you. He has no compunction about this approach because he only has to fool you for part of one evening. After the score, he doesn't plan on staying around long enough to be found out. You are a one-time diversion.

The male's usual excuse for ripping you off is that he was over-powered by his desire. While in a tumescent state he simply loses all reason and can't be held accountable.

This falsehood is easily delineated. If males really were rendered numb-brained by sexual appetite, every prostitute working would have a mansion two-blocks long and most men would be sleeping in packing crates.

Whether aroused or not, they are enough in possession of their senses to map out the surest route to physical gratification with a minimum of trouble and expense.

Arm yourself with knowledge about him. Don't be influenced by any boasts of accomplishments until you establish the truth beyond doubt. We used to have to go to the library to check a man's story and look him up in "Who's Who," "Dun And Bradstreet," or "Debrett's Peerage." But now the internet makes it easier. Any really successful man is on there somewhere, so just Google his name. If his name is a very common one, try adding his city and the name of his business to the search.

Make sure he has an on-line presence that he couldn't have created himself. Never mind what he himself wrote on Facebook, Myspace, and other public networking sites. If he's important, his name will be mentioned in on-line versions of papers of record.

Don't get intimate with a man until you have seen his home and met his family. (Not just his buddies from the bar.)

And whether or not he uses lies as a weapon for initial conquest, he is sure to use them to smooth his way throughout the affair.

Example: "I tried to call you Saturday but you didn't answer."

Naturally, you know this is false because you were waiting for his call on Saturday but it never came and he didn't show up on the caller I.D. either. The likelihood is that he had no use for you then but he's in a mood for it now so now is assuming the role of ardent suitor.

Your best strategy is *not* to let him know you know with "Gee, that's funny. I had my phone on me all day. I even carried it into the bathroom."

Instead, it's perfectly fair to counter with a lie of your own.

"Saturday? No, that's when I was invited to a party on my boss's yacht. The food and drink were sensational and there was this lingerie fashion show that sort of got out of hand. But anyhow, I wanted to invite you along and couldn't get in touch."

Another popular kind of lie is the very quickest way around your defenses, the phony marriage proposal. A predator will ask for your hand only when there is no chance of its being given, such as two hours after meeting you. Or when an actual wedding would be an impossibility. If he is stationed in the Far East, say, or doing a double-nickel in Angola.

Nothing warms a woman up faster than "proof" of a man's total commitment. And what better "proof" than the offer to

84

share his name and all his worldly goods. Though once the barriers to marriage have been removed, the eager groom will cool off, back down, start fights, and say things like, "Hey, let's not rush into this."

Another common waffle is, "You and I don't need a piece of paper to seal our relationship."

I wouldn't take possession of a *car* without "a piece of paper." Would you? A true commitment to spend your lives together should be solemnized in front of family and friends, or at least a judge.

Warning: When a man takes the trouble to be "charming," he probably wants something from you. And if he ever asks you for money for a loan or as an investment, or even twenty bucks for parking, grab your purse, take a cab home, lock the doors, and don't return his calls.

One of the predator's oldest and most successful lines is "I'm going to come into a lot of money in a few weeks. But for right now, I'm broke." Then he explains that there is a law suit pending or an insurance claim or a will being probated that will make him phenomenally wealthy. Meanwhile, Sweetums, can you handle expenses until this bounty falls on the two of you?

So you, dear girl, licking your chops, will feed, clothe, and shelter this bum in rapt anticipation of the windfall. At least until you find out it was all a ruse. But he'll stall you as long as possible with reports of temporary delays and vows to pay you back manifold. By the time you unravel all his lies and realize there is no big bonanza coming, you have been bled dry.

Instead you must reply to his plea that you're sorry but you can't possibly.

"I understand that you're going through a rough period right now. The last thing you need is a mistress draining your finances." And end the relationship.

I heard a frightening case of a woman in Massachusetts who married a man without looking into his resources. The new bride immediately had her brokerage account confiscated to settle his tax debt. Her life's savings was lost forever.

Should you have dependents, say minor children or a disabled sibling, you should have your life insured in a policy made out to them. That's being responsible. And, as your husband is your "bread-winner", you should have a policy on his life. But there is no reason in the world for your husband to have a policy on *you*. If he says it's just to be a burial policy, tell him you'll donate your body to a medical school, incurring no funeral costs.

I don't have enough space to recount all the cases of "Bluebeards" who married women, insured them up to the eyeballs, then, after a decent interval, murdered them and collected the benefit. Maybe only one man in five who gets a policy on his wife intends to knock her off to collect it. But those are bad odds anyway.

Final Note

If a man opens your acquaintance with a slightly disparaging remark, that's called a "neg" and he learned about it in "How To Pick Up Girls", a handbook for predatory men. If you're the most attractive woman in the group and he pointedly ignores you except to make mildly insulting, offhanded, remarks, he's following the steps in the book.

Beware: When the predatory male makes you a promise, he expects to be rewarded exactly as though he had already carried it out. Then, having extracted payment in advance, it would serve no purpose to actually *keep* the promise. Whether it was to mow the lawn, buy you a fur coat, or marry you.

Your best protection here is a firm policy:

Never give anything or do anything for a promise.

CHAPTER TWELVE: CONDUCTING AN AFFAIR

A woman never gets the treatment she deserves from a man. (Never!) She gets the treatment she *requires*.

You can't control the world, dearie. You probably can't even control any particular man. But you *can* control any situation as far as your own involvement in it. And this you must do from the beginning of every relationship.

Do not put up with discourtesy at the outset of your affair in the hope that Jake will treat you more decently as he grows to love you. Unfortunately, a man's manners do not improve as an association progresses. Rather, they deteriorate considerably. So make known your standard of behavior even at your first meeting.

You have the most power over the man and the situation in that brief period between his initial swell of attraction for you and the first time you take him to bed. During this interlude, he will allow all kinds of concessions toward the furtherance of his campaign. And of course this is the time to lay down your rules.

If you dislike his tobacco fumes, now is the time to forbid him to smoke in your presence. And make it clear from the start that you won't tolerate vulgar jokes or expressions. If you just grit your teeth and pretend not to mind, you will never break him of them.

Should your date be boorish enough to open his own car door first and leave you waiting alone on the sidewalk while he seats himself behind the wheel, don't just stand there meekly with the cold wind blowing up your skirt. But simply turn away and go back to your apartment, or to a cab stand.

When he does the proper thing and opens your door first and it's an old-fashioned car, naturally you will lean across and unlock his. Manners are everyone's responsibility and not just a social ritual but an essential indication of consideration and respect.

Men want and expect us women to be more civilized than they are, knowing well that if males had been allowed to establish their own living standards throughout history, they would still be sleeping in trees. (In support of this, a recent study showed that married men, on average, make 27% more money than their single counterparts. This is true even between identical twins.)

If the typical male can not devote his efforts to providing for his lady, he will lose all ambition and dissipate in time. He will drink too much, get ulcers, and drive his Pontiac into a cement wall. Why abandon the poor schmegege to this fate when you are the answer to his quest for fulfillment?

All the while, you must be demanding more from a lover than you give. And be sure to cost him more than you're worth. It's the only way to keep him interested. (One haggish and amoral femme fatale, the Duchess of Windsor, was supreme in this regard and all she cost was the crown of the British Empire.) The male ego will react in your favor here, for, in his desire to believe that he hasn't been suckered, he'll start convincing himself that you're worth more than you've been costing.

Establishing Parameters

You must discover where you stand (other than out there on that sidewalk) before wading ankle-deep into an affair. The man in question may wish to treat your liaison as casual, with no strings or demands. On *him*. But at the same time, he would like *you* to carry on as if he were the core of your entire universe.

Ideally (from his viewpoint) his practice will be to drop by your place to kill an hour after the pool hall closes. Your practice will be to greet him at the door with smiles and warm, wet kisses, convey him into the bedroom and perform every pornographic service on his inert body. After this accommodation, you will scamper into your kitchen and present him with a hearty dinner featuring red meat and gravy. You will hover over him then, watching solicitously as he enjoys it, ever alert to furnish extra portions. After he has washed down his meal with the last of your liquor, he'll pat your rump, say, "See you later." and swagger off into the night.

If you hope to protect yourself from such blatant exploitation, it is essential to press a new admirer to declare his intentions. Not about a vague future, but just from day to day. Should the boyfriend claim that he doesn't want "commitment," insist on knowing exactly what he *does* want and what he is willing to give in return. Don't settle for a foggy "Let's just see what develops." Because what may develop could be his having a sexual servant on constant call and your waiting by the phone, insecure and lonely.

Then tell him what *you* want. Don't be coy and reticent about this but state your needs clearly. Do you want this find to take you out to dinner at least three nights a week? Say so. Is he required to stay with you till morning or is a bop and run acceptable? Must he spend Christmas, New Year's, and your birthday with you? Help with the rent? Ask him point-blank whether he can afford you, then work out your terms in advance.

The dumbest thing you can do is just give him your best and assume that you will get his own best in return. The male conscience doesn't operate on a quid pro quo basis when it comes to women. He has been programmed to take and believes that, nature seeking perfect balance, you have been programmed to give. If he stops to consider whether or not this is fair, he may admit that it isn't, but biology has ordained it so.

It is absolutely astounding how selfish a man will be if you let him.

Suppose he refuses to grant you any quarter while demanding his own way on every important issue. He may even claim a kind of rakish virtue for himself with, "That's just the kind of guy I am. You want me to be honest, don't you?"

Well, sure, you want him to be honest. But you will not

accept his being selfish and insensitive. Should he grin boyish-
ly and say, "I can't change, so take me or leave me," then *leave*
him. You won't be leaving *much*.

When your masterful swain barrels into your apartment,
spreads himself out on your couch and demands to be fed, don't
think to yourself, "Oh, goody! He's bossing me around. That
must mean he loves me," and bustle off to the kitchen to show
how pleasant you can make life for an indolent. But see his
power play for what it is and stand up to it. Let no one treat you
like a servant in your own home, man, woman, or child.

If your date was hungry, he should have stopped at a restaurant and picked up something for the two of you.

It is inadvisable to cook for a man just to demonstrate your
culinary skills. This would be a waste of time and chopped
green onions. If the way to a man's heart were truly through his
stomach, then Brad Pitt would have married Rachel Ray.

The fact is that a man is not captured through a display of
the domestic arts. Yes, he will enjoy your lovingly-prepared
roasts and the warm sweaters knitted with tender care on lonely
nights. But those servile ministrations will not raise you one
quark in his estimation.

What will impress him will be your independence. The less
you need him, the more fascinated he will be.

Many women are entranced by the romantic figure of the
Geisha, that expensively-elegant Bird of Paradise who has un-
dergone years of intensive training to prepare her for a vocation
in "the art of pleasing men." She keeps an exquisite wardrobe of
kimonos, worth hundreds of thousands, and has learned to play
the samisen, perform classical dances and conduct the tea cere-
mony. She can discuss any topic of business or current events,
prettily, in a high register, and entertain her clients by popping
food into their mouths and competing in babyish games like
"scissors-rock-paper" and "musical tatami mats". Even as mature women in their seventies, they still get all dressed up in
their most expensive clothes, arrange their hair and make-up
with great care, and spend the evening being charming compa-

nions.

Though hers is perhaps the world's least feminist profession, remember that the Geisha gets several hundred dollars for an evening of dispensing charm at a banquet. She would no sooner cater to the childish male ego for free than you would spend your vacation gleefully typing quarterly reports.

This is to say you shouldn't try to ingratiate yourself to a date by lighting his cigarette, fetching his slippers, or other such obsequious gestures. You only lose a man's respect by groveling around him. And if you act like a servant, he will treat you like one, accepting your labors of love as his due.

So if you take the trouble to iron his shirt, or go to bed with him as a charity gesture (when just the very thought of it turns you green) or spend three years pulling double shifts in a meatpacking plant to put him through law school, he won't even *try* to repay you for your time and effort. Don't bother to do "wifey" things for him like brewing his coffee and washing his socks unless he's doing "husbandy" things for you. Like installing new plumbing and signing over his paychecks.

On the same tack, don't ever loan your lover money in the hope of getting it back. (Unless you're a Mafia loan shark.) He'll consider it a gift, or even think he earned it fairly by talking you out of it.

Neither should you spend your valuable time at his place when he's not interacting with you. After all, what is there to do at *his* place? Polish his collection of bowling trophies? Or just leaf through his back issues of Hustler till you vomit? There is no percentage in listening to him make business calls, or in watching him swill beer with his cronies from the pool hall, or in helping him clean his plugs and points. You could be back home practicing your guitar chords.

If you passively hang around on the furniture while he does his thing, he will soon be taking you for part of the decor while appreciating you somewhat less. When more than ten minutes pass during which he does not dedicate himself to making your visit enjoyable (even if he is in the bathroom), call a cab, go home, and do your *own* thing.

Not Making Him At Home

Don't ever give a man a key to your apartment unless he is actually living there and paying the rent. This accommodation would make you entirely too accessible.

If a man shows up uninvited, do not open your door and automatically step aside to let him in as though he has as much right in your home as you do. Keep the chain on the door instead and look at him brightly, inviting him to state his business. Just this simple tactic will make a predator ill at ease.

HIM: Uh... I thought I'd drop by and see how you were.

YOU: I'm fine. Thank you.

HIM: Well..., Aren't you going to ask me in?

YOU: For what?

(What he actually wants is to lie on your couch and watch ESPN on your large-screen T.V. while you supply him with beer and sandwiches. Later on, he would like you to gratify him during Dave's monologue. But he's not about to admit this.)

HIM: "I thought we'd spent the evening together, watching TV."

YOU: "That sounds like fun, all right. But I don't have any food in the house."

HIM: (Fuzzily) "Maybe we can... Um... grab a bite later."

YOU: "I have an even better idea. Why don't you go down to the Chinese restaurant now and pick up something for us. I would like Moo Goo Gai Pan, wonton soup, and two egg rolls."

HIM: "Eeeyah... But I didn't bring any money with me." (Never does when he expects to sponge off you.)

YOU: (Cheerily) "I understand. Maybe some other time then. Thanks for dropping by." (Now close the door and lock it.)

To forestall his wandering back in search of a free meal, don't even keep "man food" in the house. "Man food" includes cheese, especially the ones that stink to high Heaven, salami and other lunch meats, canned sardines, rye bread, relish and other components of mammoth sandwiches. Also, beer, whiskey, and anything else with an alcohol content greater than hair tonic.

Another common scenario features the man in your life saying that your relationship has lost its capacity for thrills and become burdensome. So he has decided to cool it, you should see other people, etc. Then a week or a month or a year later, lo and behold, here he comes sidling up to your door expecting to be welcomed back into your life as though you had parted on the highest of notes only the night before. Don't make it that easy for him. Again, stand in the doorway and have him state exactly what he wants.

("Well, you always were a pushover. And a date I had with this new chick fell through, so I figured I could truck on over here and get a piece without trying too hard.")

If he has hopes for resuming the affair, work out the terms before opening that door. He can pass his credit card over the chain or sign a check. (He must write in the memo, "Repayment of Loan" so if he stops payment, you can still pursue him for the amount in court.) And ascertain that your requirements have been met *before* you give him anything. Even a smile or a sandwich.

Behaving

While in the thick of a romance, you mustn't tolerate gestures any more intimate than hand-holding in public. Necking at a party is not only vulgar, but it also gives the impression that, for the most sinister or pathetic of reasons, you haven't any place to bring the guy. And no one thinks well of a woman who acts over-sexed for a crowd, as these torrid charades suggest she would be happy to take on any and everybody, not just the one she's presently consorting with. So keep his flaming passion corked until you get him alone.

Never Stop Preventing

When the man in your life tries to talk you out of using contraceptives, this does *not* mean that he wishes to become a father. More probably, he would like to see proof of his virility and will send you off to an abortionist as soon as the evidence is in. He has little to lose from this experiment. It isn't *his* body that has to be pried open and excavated.

There is a related breed of rat who enjoys the begetting of children but not the raising or supporting of them. He will impregnate you with one foot on the bus, in a manner of speaking. If your consort has any children, anywhere, he doesn't support, he's one of these. (And don't listen to his griping about his nasty, profligate, ex-wife. It's a man's responsibility to provide for his children whether he likes their mother or not. Whether she is re-married or not.)

So don't fall prey to his urge to multiply.

Is He Worth It?

About a month or so into your affair, you should evaluate the association and decide whether the factors you entered it for (money, companionship, social connections or whatever) have been delivered to your satisfaction. What substantial benefit have you derived to date? If you're still going on hopes and promises, cut your losses now and pack it in. Enough time wasted.

Does He Love You? Don't answer too quickly. Perhaps he loves to go to bed with you. Or he loves your flattering his ego. It could be that he loves the meals you cook him and the way you iron his shirts. But still he may not love *you.*

Women have a penchant for self-deception here via some tortuous arguments. Like "I'm positive he loves me because he always buys me a nice present after he beats me up."

This won't do!

One way to get a handle on the truth is to ask your best friend, Edna. She has seen the way "Mr. Right" has been treating you and can form a shrewd and objective conclusion as to his sincerity. But while you're waiting to get a call through to Edna, here are a few telling indications of his devotion or lack of it:

He may love you if:

He wants to spend every night with you.

He gives you his paychecks.

Your engagement ring is a carat or more.

He gave up smoking/drinking/gambling at your request.

He loved your family, sight unseen.

He brought you home to his own family and introduced you as his fiancée.

He volunteers for chores around your house.

You have the free use of his car,

You're not afraid to send him out for hemorrhoid suppositories.

On the other hand, he certainly does *not* love you if:

After intercourse, he is abrupt and anxious to get rid of you.

He sees you no more than two or three times a week and sex is always part of the program.

He never has time for you when you're menstruating.

You feel that you have to look your best for him at all times.

He's "regardant." (Always looking to make sure he gets as much as he gives.)

He spends more time/money on his car than on you.

You're not married, but he wants to have sex without protection.

He says, "I love you *but*..."

He buys you a vaginal deodorant.

When analyzing the quality of his feelings, consider whether you are an important part of the whole of his life or merely the whole of *one* part of it. The greater the ratio of "other" activities to sexual activities in your time together, the more compatible you are and the better your chance for a constructive long-term association. If most of your time together is spent in bed or on the way to or from a bed, this isn't a "relationship" at all. And unless you're receiving a substantial consideration for your time and effort, you are being "had" figuratively as well as literally.

If a man calls you late some night, drunk, to say he's been thinking about you a lot lately and wants to come over and see you right away, just hang up.

We used to call what he has in mind a "quickie". In the seventies, Erica Jong came up with the term "Zipless F**k" which I don't understand. (I mean, how do you do it without unzipping anything?) Now there is a vulgar new term for that vulgar exertion, a "booty call."

If your man wants you to dominate him in bed, even acts like an abject and whimpering slave there but treats you like dirt when you're both upright, you're much the loser, sister.

Ruling in bed doesn't count!

Should the brief checklist above and other factors indicate that the man in your scope is not giving you the care and attention you deserve, hunt elsewhere.

If you are already living with this putz, go ahead and move out. Don't prepare him for the event with forewarning, either. But simply allow him to return to his pad tomorrow night to find it stripped of all feminine trappings and you gone. Slipping out with all your gear is a lot of bother but it's effective.

He will probably be on the phone to your mother, sobbing that he now realizes the immensity of his love for you and coming around to your job, kneeling in the parking lot, whining promises to mend his ways if only you will make his house a home again. Before agreeing to return, you must get a substantial token of his sincerity, like a wedding ring or an office building.

Your only risk in leaving is that the slug may discover that he can get along just fine without you. If this be the case, you haven't split a minute too soon.

(You aren't getting any younger, you know.)

By the way, if you were foolish enough to spend your own money fixing up his home in the mistaken assumption it would be yours for life, you may *not* tear out the hot tub or the garden fountain you had installed. They are now "fixed" parts of his property and may not be removed.

Even if you haven't been living with this unloving man, absence is still the ticket. Buy one. To Alaska which is loaded with single men, or maybe Martha's Vineyard for the summer or London for the theater season. Or as far as you can go. If actual travel is impossible, you can still "disappear" for your own intents and purposes. Go visit old friends; make new ones; join a chorus. Take courses in something. Get involved and unavailable. If you quit the man cold turkey, you will all the sooner free yourself of an unhealthy preoccupation with him.

Then you will be well-rested and renewed for a more loving and worthy sort.

"Heaven has no rage like love to hatred turned. Nor Hell a fury like a woman scorned." William Congreve in "The Mourning Bride".

CHAPTER THIRTEEN:
BREAKING UP BROKEN DOWN

When A Lover Dumps You

After several months or years of giving your time, love, body, and maybe even cash to a man, he is as likely as not to get restless and decided to end your relationship "before it gets too serious."

(The most beautiful and glamorous women in history were rejected by men they loved, so don't think it can't happen to you.)

Once he has made this decision, there will be no changing his mind, as you have already lost any emotional power over him. By the time he delivers his well-rehearsed speech about "needing his own space" and "seeing other people" it will do you no good to have hysterics so be cool and serene.

If the guy is rich, pull yourself together and try to make the best of the debacle. This pinhead may have a little residual guilt and a little decorous weeping could move him to give you a nice property settlement. This must be in writing of course, even if you have to get it on a cocktail napkin with the waitress witnessing the signature.

To wit: "In compensation for her two years of domestic and personal services and other considerations, and in exchange for her renouncing all additional claims on my property, I, John Doe, will turn over to Jane Roe stocks and securities totaling $250,000 in market value. I will also make her an allowance of five thousand a month for one year or until she marries."

Better make that a *dinner* napkin, and the waitress *and* the bartender.

Because as soon as he's well rid of you, Mr. Rat will want to renege on any promises. He'd like to keep all his money for the new girl.

Ask him to introduce you to his rich friend, Louis.

You might offer to sell him back the expensive presents he gave you. Do not, under any circumstances, offer to *give* them back. You accepted them in good faith and are not an Indian taker. If a mere boyfriend without resources says he wants to break up with you, for whatever reason, you must agree with him immediately. There is no sense in letting him know how much he's hurt you. Meet his kiss-off speech with emphatic agreement. Tell him it's long been obvious that your feelings for each other have gone stale. You had been trying to find a way to tell him this but were afraid of causing a scene. And you are delighted that he had the courage to bring it up.

"Oh, Robert, I'm so relieved that you said it first. I blame myself. I had this fantasy image of you as some brilliant, macho, hero, the answer to all my prayers. And I didn't want to admit how disappointed I had become. Of course we shouldn't see each other again." Pat his shoulder and smile gratefully. "Now I don't have to put off my trip to Martha's Vineyard!"

Then *go* take a weekend at a Bed & Breakfast on Martha's Vineyard or museum-hopping in New York or fishing off Cape Hatteras or to whichever place or pursuit he might envy.

If he treats you badly at the break-up, you might take other steps.

Put pin holes in the tops of all his beers.

E-mail his boss the digital photo you took of him wearing your bra.

Take his wife to lunch, tell her the whole story, and offer to testify as co-respondent if she wants to file for divorce.

Of course the best revenge is not caring at all. Consider that you won the match. He lost *you.* You only lost *him.*

Pulling Yourself Together

Don't try drinking to get over a man. Alcohol doesn't douse a flame, but fuels it. Pig out on chocolate instead. It contains Phenylethylamine, the same stimulating chemical your brain releases when you're madly in love.

Remind yourself that there was never born a man you can't live without.

Cross stitch the motto, "He's not worth it." on a sampler and hang it over your desk.

Sit down and figure out in which ways the defector had been making your life better. Then think of ways to achieve the same advantages without him.

If he has been taking you sailing, you can find other friends with boats or rent a boat.

If he's been taking you to great restaurants, you can go with a friend, or cook the dishes yourself.

A few accessories and provisions can make you forget you ever had any use for the larger and smellier sex:

Aluminum siding or weatherboard on your house will save you the trouble of painting it every few years.

Buy a rubber gripper to open jars. A dishwashing glove also works.

Take a course in auto mechanics at your local community college.

A small step ladder will enable you to reach everything high up.

Get yourself a roll of duct tape, a crescent wrench, pliers, a hammer, and a set of screw drivers: Phillips and flat head. Almost any handyman's task can be accomplished with these. (To get a screw in, you have to make a "pilot" hole with a nail first. Every man seems to know this.)

Electric blankets are very reasonable, but cuddly dogs are even better. They keep you warmer than men do, take up less room, and smell better.

Use a pocket calculator to balance your checkbook. Pay a

C.P.A. at tax time.

There are devices to change the pitch of one's voice on the phone. (The iPhone has an "app" for this.) These are mainly used by big hairy, men who have to sound like cute young girls to work as phone sex operators. But for those occasions when you need "an authoritative male voice" to get action from contractors, you might use one to make yourself sound like a big, hairy, man on the phone.

You should also take an assertiveness training course and study up on consumer rights so you can be an "authoritative female voice."

Buy a quick-starting charcoal for barbecues and easy-burning logs for the fireplace.

Waitresses often give women bad service because we have a reputation for being stingy tippers. Don't you be. When dining out, always demand a good table and good service, then tip well. The staff will remember you next time and treat you as courteously as any man.

Put your own garbage out before it gets dark.

Don't buy dresses or bras you have to fasten in the back.

Get the Wall Street Journal and learn to read stock quotations.

Saw the first foot off an old broom handle.

And have such a fabulous life for yourself that he is miserable to no longer be a part of it.

Now curl up by your stereo and listen to the first part of Beethoven's String Quartet in C Sharp Minor, Opus 131.

Because maybe all you really need is a good fugue.

When You Want To Dump A Lover

Before he suspects your intentions, unobtrusively pick up and spirit away all the belongings you have been keeping at his place.

If you can't casually swipe back your own apartment key, change the tumbler mechanism on your lock. A new one will cost you about six bucks at a hardware store and take you a screw driver and a couple of minutes to install. You can do it during a station break.

Make recordings of all his best albums.

Gather up all the photos he took of you in better times and destroy the filthy ones.

Get your teeth fixed on his company dental plan.

Copy important names and numbers from his address book.

Have all charge accounts switched over to your own name. If you can't do that, charge up to the limit before he cuts off your credit.

If he is using a cell phone in your name, cancel it now, even though you have to pay a cancellation fee.

Get any expensive gifts he has given you out of sight, preferably at your mother's, so he can't go on a rampage throughout your apartment reclaiming them all. Hell, you *earned* them.

Put all his personal belongings in a neat, portable, pile near the door so he won't have to go looking for them. And give him a sack to carry them in.

Have a relative or girlfriend (not a boyfriend) on the premises to discourage an awkward scene. If the one being ousted has ever shown a violent streak, the relative should be a large and nasty one.

Matters are more complicated when the dumpee is already living with you.

If the lease is in your name alone you may be free to evict him. But check that point with a lawyer first. If the dumpee won't stay evicted, you can get a restraining order.

Should you decide to move yourself out, choose some clear morning after he has left for work. If you don't have an able-bodied friend with a truck, you can rent a U-Haul van and dolly. The van will have an automatic transmission and a ramp and you and your mom can clear out the joint inside of an hour.

If your living mate has kept you so destitute that you haven't enough cash to rent a truck, you can raise it by pawning his gun collection. Or put a blind ad in the penny saver to sell his wardrobe and metal detector.

If there is nothing in that apartment worth pawning or selling, what are you still doing there?

"Women have a need to 'nest' more than men do. So women are willing to settle for less than they deserve." Judge Judy Sheindlin

CHAPTER FOURTEEN: CHOOSING MARRIAGE

Almost from infancy, we're inundated with propaganda extolling marriage as our ultimate goal. But before succumbing to this insidious pressure, stop and consider what you actually have to gain from the conjugal state. Not security, I'm afraid, since about half of marriages end in divorce. And you shouldn't go into it for companionship either. If you want silent company, a cat would be a better choice than a man. It will also eat less and keep mice away.

If what you desire is conversation, then marriage is absolutely wrong for you. Give a listen to a typical husband's "conversation."

"Hey! Where's my clean t-shirt?"

"Get the dog out of here!"

And "You wouldn't believe my pool game today. Even while I was racking the balls, I had this good feeling about it and..." (Forty-five minutes of excruciatingly boring description follows.)

If you just want a long-term association with a man, it's best to keep it informal. The ending of it will be cheaper and less traumatic that way. Don't forget, either, that if you marry many times, your promiscuity becomes a matter of public record. And you get to looking like some ding-bat who can't keep her life in order.

Now, before you walk down the aisle with that three-legged nuisance, examine your real motive for making the trip. Don't lie to yourself either. What you really want is to be taken care of, right?

And why not. Here you are slogging away at some crummy job in a flange factory. You get up at six-thirty, ride a crowded and jerking bus, wedged among seventy-eight other *poor* people, work your shift with grinding teeth, hate your supervisor, and trudge home after dark for a paltry $324 a week take-home pay.

So you're thinking, "Boy, I've *had* it with this scene. Bob makes twice the money I do, so I'll just marry him, quit working, and live in comfort."

Okay, hold it right there!

Stop and look ahead a few years. Let us imagine your future as an employee with the flange factory and contrast that with your prospects if you throw in with Bob. There are several categories to be surveyed.

Time

With the flange factory: Work takes up fifty hours a week, including the commute. That leaves one-hundred and eighteen hours for you.

With Bob: Cooking, cleaning, grocery shopping and laundry occupy most of your time. During the hundred odd hours per week Bob is at home, you are on call to tote his food and drink including between-meal meals. You are also obligated to listen without seeming bored as he describes trivial aspects of his work in great and soporific detail. You may manage to salvage ten hours a week to pursue your own interests. He will expect you to feel guilty about this.

Money

With the flange factory: You get promoted to supervisor with a substantial raise. You acquire stock options and an IRA account. You save some, spend some, waste some. But it's all yours.

With Bob: It soon transpires that Bob wasn't making quite as much as he let on before the wedding. Also, he is still paying for the Trans Am he totaled the week before you met. What little he does bring home is spent on food. It seems he needs a hot breakfast every morning, a full-course dinner every night, and Dagwood sandwiches in between. His largest expenditure is for beer, enough of which he drinks to float a pipe-laying barge. Bob doesn't believe in letting women handle money. Your income is whatever change you can glean from his pants pockets while he sleeps. You also dig under chair cushions.

Social Life
With the factory: After hours drinks with co-workers, club meetings, evening classes, weekend tennis lessons, charter flights with your alumni association.

With Bob: You kidding? Bob won't tolerate any of your friends and he has none of his own except his backward, mutant, brother, "Squirrel". A trip to the laundromat is as much of an outing as you get. Yesterday, the landlady came by to complain that Bob's rent check had bounced again and you made her a cup of coffee just to have someone to talk to.

Entertainment
With the factory: A season ticket to the local theater group, concerts, an occasional ballet or opera.

With Bob: You have seen every film Ray Milland ever made on basic cable.

Sex
With the factory: Love affairs of varying heat and duration. Perhaps there are long fallow periods. But the choice of whether or not to participate is always your own.

With Bob: Ugh! Unfortunately, all that beer he puts away dulls his prowess but not his appetite for sex. You have forgotten what you ever liked about it and think if you never see another one you won't miss it. This is the most unpleasant of your household duties and, as he flails away, you wish you were back in the kitchen peacefully hunched over a sink full of grea-

106

sy dishes.

Assets After Six Years

With the factory: a substantial nest egg in a Mutual Fund, car almost paid for, pension plan, new entertainment center, fine wardrobe, coordinated and added to over the years, furniture and appliances, savings account...

With Bob: It is statistically valid to figure that here is where the love nest breaks up. You can no longer pretend to be thrilled with Bob and he's getting tired of waking up in the same bed every morning.

So here is the sum of your assets after six years:

An old analog TV.

An old hide-away bed that stays in hiding.

Two hundred and three dollars in the bank. (Combed from the lint of chair cushions.)

The winter coat your mother bought you your last year of high school.

Now, do you want to go back and start over?

Very well, then. Bob was a bad bargain and so are most members of the opposing sex. This is because the human male was bred to be selfish and domineering. The beast in question can be partially domesticated only if he is so smitten with a woman that he is eager to subordinate his will to hers.

On entering the matrimonial state, be aware that the unwritten contract is geometrically more important than the legal one. Determine what your intended wants of you and you of him before you sign up for life. Perhaps the bargain, as he understands it, provides that you remain a size eight and continue to be as chic, soigné, and youthful as you are today. Even after childbirth and motherhood. Maybe he expects you to hold down a full-time job as well, so if you think you can retire to a life of tranquil domesticity, you're in for a disagreeable surprise. Make sure it's no surprise.

Establish your own rules too. You like your intended just

fine as a dynamic young stock broker. So if he gets the idea that he might quit the rat race to become a poor but proud camp counselor, he can just forget it right now.

And don't marry any man unless you thereby gain something you can't have without marrying him.

"Marriage and hanging go by destiny; matches are made in Heaven." Robert Burton.

CHAPTER FIFTEEN: CHOOSING A HUSBAND

Husbands tend to be grossly over-sized creatures who require about three times the living space as an average woman. Most of them over-eat, get drunk often, stumble around breaking things, make incessant demands on your attention, go for days without shaving, burp loudly (which they think an expression of wit) and leave the toilet seat up. Also, they have loud, booming voices, pitched for issuing demands, and prodigious amounts of intestinal gas.

Males are flawed in most ways that count. When visiting the home of a single woman, you will most likely see a cozy little nest she has feathered for herself with color-coordinated draperies and slip covers.

Now steel yourself to look in on the lair of a single, hetero, male. If he's poor, it will resemble Deke House on New Year's Day, with dirty linen kicked into the corners, piles of car parts in the bedroom, and plates of mold and fungus in the kitchen sink. If the man is rich, his place will convey the "Sam Giancana Suite" at a motel on the Vegas strip.

Consider also that the husband may make more demands of your time and resources than an eight-year-old child. Sure, the child needs rides to girl scouts and piano lessons and constant supervision of its eating and study habits. But the kid won't demand that you jump up and fetch it a beer every twelve minutes or call you away from your work to hunt for an auto repair manual or badger you for sex when you're too tired even to *spit*.

Now... Are you sure you want one?

But before you get the idea that we can live without them,

consider another side of the male aggression factor. That same pernicious trait that moves men to start wars, exceed speed limits, and brag about real or pretend conquests, has a positive application. Men are so eager to prove their power and virility that they sometimes do very useful things to earn the respect of their peers. Like discover vaccines, build bridges, and invent television.

Bad Choices

First, with Pollyannic optimism, we must rule out the most outrageous of the intolerables.

It is often said that a woman doesn't appreciate a good man when she gets one because he isn't "thrilling" enough. Sadly, this is true of many of us. The immature and uninformed (dumb) woman fantasizes being swept off her feet by the likes of Bronte's "Heathcliff" who will love her violently and obsessively. She longs to be consumed by smoldering dark eyes and dangerous gypsy passions. Exciting? Sure. But so are earthquakes and forest fires.

If you read "Wuthering Heights" all the way through, you will recall what a rotten husband "Heathcliff" turned out to be. Violent Gypsy passions may be a kick for one frenetic weekend in Dubrovnik. But the realities of daily life back home in Gasport would very quickly douse those flames.

The same animal magnetism that makes some men so sexy and fascinating also renders them impossible to live with. That heart-stirring physical tension vibrating beneath the surface often erupts into cruel callousness, even brutality. And a broken nose doesn't look good on anybody.

You will have a better chance for a successful marriage if you realize at the start that it's not your husband's responsibility to keep you in a perennial state of quivering excitement.

Understand that we're not considering a lover in this chapter but a life-long legal partner. So we're not looking for thrills here but for a nice, dull fellow who will come straight home from the office, turn over his paychecks, and do his share of the housework. (Say, eighty percent.) Dark and dangerous obsessions have no place in a home.

To protect yourself from the horror and destruction of a bad match, it is imperative *not* to marry a man you are "in love" with. To forestall being enslaved by your imagination, or your baser appetites, it would help to realize that while erotic attraction may be a *good* reason to have an affair, it is also a *bad* reason to get married. Do not make any legal commitment, least of all a nuptial one, to a man you have a crush on. This form of temporary insanity numbs the judgment and renders you powerless to make an informed decision.

And you're liable to wake up five months from now, all alone in Agnew, Nebraska, with empty pockets, a throbbing headache, and a foul taste in your mouth.

Marry for money, position, a rent-controlled apartment, discount tickets... They'll all outlast passion.

If being with a man or kissing him causes a stirring in your... uh... heart, that may be a hormonal reaction or a memory of a former lover. It is *not* a sign from God that you should marry this person, have his children, and live with him forever.

As explained in another chapter, the feeling of being "in love" is only a fleeting condition indicative of nothing except, maybe, hormones. But it will so distort your perception of its object that you will be unfit to make an intelligent decision about his qualifications for a connubial life.

Mind you, a man who is too easy to marry probably isn't worth marrying. Do a credit check before accepting his ring.

And don't choose a man on the basis of how "wonderful" he is. Consider instead what "wonderful" things he can do for *you*.

Marriage of woman to man is an inevitable component of the human condition, and there are many reasons why the male and female complement each other so well. It may seem ludicrous that nature endowed the members of the more selfish and destructive gender with superior strength. But if it weren't for their muscle power, we women would have no use for the poor beasts at all.

It is nature's plan that men do the hard physical work and make most of the technological advances while women exert the civilizing and socially-conscious influence. He builds the house; she makes it a home.

Your mission, should you choose to accept it, is to channel one man's energy and ambition toward humanitarian aims.

Males are constructed to perform tasks requiring great physical expenditure (like digging ditches) while we females are better fitted for sedentary work. (Like running a corporation.)

Evidence of this divergence is easily observed in the lives of share-croppers. Men who spend their lives tilling the soil, as nature intended, seem to thrive and grow attractively rugged under the burning sun. While the wretched women who are unnaturally forced to work beside them become dried and wrinkled crones by age forty. Certainly the male sex has almost obsoleted itself now that its hard-won technology has made muscular might a matter of little relevance.

If you are still determined to bag one of the creatures for yourself, then at least choose your game wisely.

In order to handle a man you must get a "handle" *on* him. That is, find out what he needs that you can provide better than anyone else could, or would. If he has no such "handle" for you to control him by, then don't waste your time or your best years, on a hopeless case.

Most straight men who have remained unmarried past the age of forty have been left that way for an excellent reason. They're losers! Most old bachelors are so cheap that they still live with their mothers. And they let Mom cut their hair which is why they look like Owen Wilson after a long swim. They aren't up to the responsibility of a wife, of a stable lifestyle, or a presentable habitat.

If your prospective spouse has a minor or disabled child he isn't supporting, run away. If he has a non-minor, non-disabled child he *is* supporting, look very carefully. All his resources may be going to a dissolute, favorite kid, leaving none for you. Some otherwise-promising men are actually worthless because their grown children have a stranglehold on their affections and their bank accounts. Once a man's children are out of graduate school, *you* should be his priority, not they.

Most straight men feel a need for a woman's love. Those who don't are either inmates or astonishingly undersexed. An undersexed man is difficult to handle, because if he wants it less than you do, you have no leverage with him. You can't use sexual extortion to get your way and quarrels may drag on for weeks.

His Family

If your prospective mother-in-law is a nasty old bitch, just avoid her. She's not going to leave you her money in any case, right?

But if his *kids* hate you, don't marry him. They'll make your life Hell and leech away all his money to boot.

Don't Marry Old

It's natural to want a "daddy" to take care of you. You long to curl up in his lap for a cuddle as this loving oracle delivers resolutions to all of life's problems a la "Father Knows Best." And his libido has declined to the point where he isn't all over you like a squid when you want to be left alone. He makes you feel young, girlish, and secure.

But there is a gigantic drawback. The older man's heart has atrophied. His emotions are so dried up that he's not capable of romantic love anymore, so he eschews the discomfort and inconvenience of the grand amour. Pops may be happy to keep you around so long as you conform to his inflexible lifestyle. But once you begin to make physical and emotional demands, you'll be frozen out. Whereas a young cock will run all over town at two in the morning to find your favorite brand of peanut

113

brittle, the tired old bird won't even stir out of his recliner to toss you a Mason Mint when you're dying of an insulin fit.

Don't be fooled if the older man still looks handsome and fit. A good thirty years can pass between his complete loss of attractiveness and the time he finally croaks.

Sure, he may have more money than your contemporaries. But after a certain age, the proctologist gets it all anyhow.

Fifteen years ago, a friend I'll call "Elmo" married a girl twenty-four years his junior. "Bunny" thought him a good catch at the time as he was better-educated than the boys she had been dating and made more money. And he was proud to show her off at family picnics, a nubile testament to his virility. Their happiness was complete all the way through the honeymoon. Then the first area of incompatibility cropped up as Bunny, like most young women, felt a need for children. Elmo had already raised a family and purely didn't welcome the trouble and expense, but his lovely bride popped out three hyperactive little darlings in the next six years. The money Elmo had been saving for a leisurely retirement was dribbled away on diapers, toys, and Ritalin.

Today, Elmo is sixty, retired on disability with a slew of health problems, and getting grumpier by the day. Bunny, still pretty at thirty-six, sometimes runs into old school mates, now handsome, successful men in their prime, and thinks she would like to go out and have fun some time, socialize, maybe even have sex again with someone who's able.

Her decrepit husband desires nothing more than to sit quietly in his recliner and watch the History Channel. But the children run through the house, whooping like movie Indians, blasting their CDs and practicing their trumpets.

I haven't seen Elmo smile in years.

Here's another true-life example: My neighbor, Tina, was twenty-three when she married a handsome divorcé in his forties. Dom owned the most profitable restaurant in town and drove a Cadillac.

At the time, I thought Tina had done well for herself by

skipping the "struggling newlywed" phase of life and latching on to a man who had already made it. But Dom turned out not to be the "catch" she assumed because, like most men his age, he had already sired a family and was still paying for the split-level they were living in. And his kids were almost ready for college, incurring *those* toe-curling expenses. The Cadillac was past its prime and not performing as expected. (Apply appropriate metaphor.)

Tina thought she deserved her own split level and the other perks appropriate to the wife of a successful man including children, so produced two of those within four years. Supporting two complete families cost Dom more than he was making, so he began taking too much money out of the restaurant, put in more tables, and bought cheaper food to serve. The restaurant lost its following and went bankrupt. Then, for good measure, Dom fell victim to early-onset Alzheimer's. So nowadays, Tina works long hours as a bookkeeper in a tire store to support her family, then goes home and plays nursemaid to her blathering, befuddled, husband.

Understand that the "struggling newlywed" phase can be the best time of your life, if you're healthy, in love, and not trying to support children.

Do not marry an older man for his money unless he is so old and sick that his demise is imminent and he'll leave you a fortune. (Nice paycheck.) Or you can have the old coot committed and get named his conservator.

Men According To Profession

A woman with strong career ambitions is likely to encounter two different kinds of suitors with their respective marriage proposals.

GUY 1: "You'll never make it in that career anyway, so forget the whole thing and marry me."

GUY 2: "Marry me and I'll *help* you make it."

Even a clam brain will understand that the first type is to be plowed under and the second to be gratefully cultivated.

Do not commit yourself to a man who will expect you to mold your life around his. Instead, decide where your own ambitions lie and choose a husband who will help you achieve them. If you want to be a lawyer, for example, take a law school professor, a senior partner in a law firm, or a judge. Do not marry a bookie or a petty gangster, however cute.

Get the idea?

If you want to be an actress, marry an agent, director, producer, or possibly just some devoted dear who lives in New York or L.A. and will subsidize your acting lessons and auditioning expenses until you make it. Do not marry the leading citizen of Sheboygan, Wisconsin, or anyone else who doesn't live in an entertainment capital.

If you would like to design dresses, look for a fabric manufacturer, an accountant, or a public relations man. You don't want a forest ranger or a homophobe.

An aspiring physician should take up with the dean of a medical school, chief of staff at a major hospital, or an expert on tax shelters. Contra-indicated are clinging, possessive, men who make demands on her time, and Christian Scientists.

A would-be airline pilot should find herself an owner of a flight school or a vice-president of a growing airline. She doesn't need a Mormon who wants twelve kids. (Neither does anyone else.)

If you want to be a stock-broker, marry Merrill, Lynch, Pierce, Fenner, or Smith. Don't take anyone who subscribes to a racing form.

A woman who (Ghack!) feels her vocation in life is to be a housewife and mother needs a strong, healthy, young stud with nerves of steel, infinite patience, and a depression-proof job who loves children and fixing things around the house. She doesn't need a natural loner, a footloose type, or a man with any genetic defects. Like ugliness.

And the poor fool of a woman who decides upon a writing career had better marry a man who can support her for a very long time.

White vs. Blue

Taking the overview, white collar men work at sit-down jobs which they know any woman can do as well, so they have a problem with their masculine identity. And they sometimes compensate for this manque by becoming insufferably dictatorial at home. They're also more prone to bouts of impotence than their blue-collar counterparts.

White-collar men tend to be pale and cowardly wimps, but they try to keep themselves in shape at a health club. Also, they shave regularly and are presentable for dinners out and the like. They usually know what year it is, and even the month, because they use dates in their work.

On the minus side, the white collar family is at the mercy of trades people. When your basement pipes leak, they will spritz and spatter for days or weeks at the whim of your plumber. And the replacement of a two-foot length of PVC will cost you about a week's salary. When your soft, office-bound husband limps his Buick sedan into a service station to complain about "that scary, knocking sound," the auto mechanic will be on the phone ordering tickets to Las Vegas before Hubby is even out of his car.

The blue-collar man, by contrast, will be very masculine and ruggedly handsome in his youth. Trouble is, he has no vanity and deteriorates steadily over the years. If he drinks a lot of beer, he will develop a gross beer belly and a bulbous nose by the age of fifty. The hair cuts he gets from his father's barber don't help either. Or that he owns but one suit. (It's bright blue polyester.) And you can't show him to your friends.

The blue collar man is usually a rotten conversationalist. His purview gets narrower with each passing decade, till he is cognizant of nothing but shop and sports. His manners are atrocious and he is incapable of talking to your women friends except in grunts. You will be happy to leave him at home.

One advantage is that the blue collar man doesn't mind when you lose your looks either. A few extra pounds around your hips he may refer to as "more to love." He is less inclined to leave you for a younger woman than his white collar counterpart as he hasn't the appeal or the imagination.

Another plus is that he can probably tune your car engine. And that burst pipe in the cellar will be replaced within the hour, after a quick trip to a plumbing supply house. Tradesmen respect their working class peers too and are less likely to try to cheat them. The money you save in this area will put you well ahead of most families headed by a college graduate.

Men According To Sun Signs

"I Am"

If your guy is a Ram: Since Aries rules the head, he is likely to be handsome, but is usually thoughtless of the concerns of others if they don't jibe with his plans to put himself first. Marlon Brando was an Aries. Not only was he gorgeous to look at but he was a "first," a pioneer in his method of acting. Other Aries "pioneers" in their various fields are: Giovanni Casanova, Butch Cassidy, Francis Ford Coppola, and William Shatner.

"I Possess"

Taurus men tend to be comfortable and materialistic which are good qualities for a husband, but bulls are usually stick-on-the-couch boring at home. Some famous Taureans are Dwayne Johnson, Tony Blair, George Clooney, and Craig Ferguson.

"I Communicate"

The men of the sign of the Twins are skilled at chit-chat but have the attention span of a flea at a dog show. Not to say they are shallow, but you can go wading in most Geminis and not get your toenails wet. They may enjoy talking about sex and thinking about sex more than actually engaging in it. Some glib Geminis are Donald Trump, Chris Elliot, Hugh Laurie, and Michael J. Fox.

"I Root"

Cancer is the sign of hospitality and all things domestic, including food and real estate. (Back in the sixties, the term "Cancer" gave rise to such unpleasant images of disease that they started calling its natives "Moon Children". Whoever decides these things eventually came to realize that "Moon Children" sounds worse.)

If your man is a crab, he is probably a homebody. But he may be so sensitive that he takes everything personally and you have to watch what you say around him. Some famous Cancerians are: Tom Cruise, Harrison Ford, Nelson Mandela, and Robin Williams.

"I Create"

Leo directs creations of the body and creations of the mind. Its ruler is the Sun, the center of the solar system. If your guy is a lion, don't tell him you want to talk about *yourself*. He's having these problems that are the most important concerns in the world. Leos like to be prominent and hold the title of "King" but usually don't want all the work and responsibility that come with real leadership. On the positive side, they're good fathers. Fidel Castro, Don Imus, Fred Dalton Thompson, and Shimon Peres are some Leo "Kings of the realm."

"I Analyze"

If we all were Virgos, con men couldn't make a living. It's the sign of shrewd analysis.

It's also the sign of habits, good and bad. Poor Virgos are still smoking long after everyone else in their social sphere has given it up.

You want your doctor to be a Virgo because if there's any little thing wrong with you, he'll tell you what it is. You may not want your husband to be a Virgo because if there's any little thing wrong with you, he'll tell you what it is.

Some meticulous Virgo men are Prince Harry, Tommy Lee Jones, James Gandolfini, and Hugh Grant.

"I Relate"

Libra is a very fortunate sign because it's ruled by Venus in its expression of love and beauty. Those born under the sign of

119

the scales tend to have good looks and charm and can usually get their way by manipulating others. Libra men are great at *starting* relationships, but they won't make any adjustments to keep one going, because it's easier just to start a new one. The joke is "Librans marry early and often." And they love debate for its own sake; that's why they make good litigators. Some charming Libras are Sting, Tony Shalhoub, Clive Owen, and Liev Schreiber.

"I Merge"

Scorpio is the most powerful sign and rules the inevitables: sex, death, and taxes. (The Scorpio men who have come on to me were all either cheap or carrying a sexually-transmitted disease.) The late, great, actor, Richard Burton, was a poster Scorpio: a stingy, drunken, sex addict. Some good and bad Scorpions include Kevin Kline, Sam Waterston, Larry Flynt, and John Gotti.

"I Expand"

Sagittarius, ruled by the greater benefic, Jupiter, is the most fortunate sign which favors travel, publishing, and higher education. If you're interested in a male Archer, understand that freedom and independence are more important to him than any relationship. Don't try to hold on tight. Far-reaching Sag men are: Don Johnson, John Kerry, Jon Stewart, and Brad Pitt.

"I Ascend"

Capricorn is ruled by Saturn who decrees that you have to work very hard for everything you get. But once you get it, you're allowed to keep it. Old Man Saturn runs a celestial employment agency to make sure that all of his subjects are gainfully occupied at all times. The pessimistic goats have a great ability to work hard and concentrate and almost always move upward from the circumstances of their birth. Capricorn is the sign of endurance and natives tend to stay in marriages long after they've ceased to be any good. Some hard-working men born under the sign are Denzel Washington, Rod Stewart, Mario Van Peebles, and Ryan Seacrest.

"I Evolve"

Aquarius is the sign of high technology, new age science, and alternative everything. Water-bearers are ruled by far-out Uranus, the only planet that "rolls on its belly", that is turns horizontally instead of vertically like the others. Aquarians believe they were dumped on earth from some far-off planet with a vastly more evolved civilization. The Aquarian male isn't materialistic enough to apply himself to making a good living. He is too "evolved" to slog away at some mundane job just to provide the modern comforts. Galileo, Havelock Ellis, Alan Alda, and Eddie Izzard were born counter-culture Aquarians .

"I Transcend"

Pisces is the sign that bestows the most intuitive talent and also illusions. Many men born under this sign make promises they have no way of keeping. They assume that just the promise itself has currency and you should treat them as well as if they had delivered on it. The very stars which make them so creative also make them vulnerable to addictions. Jerry Lewis, Michael Caine, Patrick Duffy ("The Man From Atlantis"), and Kelsey Grammar are fish.

Sub-Groups

Having categorized men by class and sign, we may as well assess some of their ethnic identifications too.

Disclaimer: While no generalization applies to all individuals in any group, it can be observed that certain traits run in certain nationalities.

WASPs: Bland as he is, the Protestant can be an ideal partner. But you have to like dogs; he's sure to have one. (And it's a *big* mother, too.) The WASP may wear a suit and tie during the week and probably has a workshop in the garage which will keep him happily out of your hair most evenings. He shaves even on weekends when he takes the kids grocery shopping in the SUV.

IRISHMEN: Hopeless! The Hibernian believes sex to be a mortal sin. That is, if it's done *right* it's a mortal sin. But if the reprehensible act is conducted with a minimum of enjoyment and got over with quickly, maybe it's only a *venial* sin. Don't hope you can teach this unfortunate to please you. By the time he has graduated from a Jesuit-run college, he has been ruined.

Irishmen, however, do have the gift of blarney and are the greatest wits in the world. So I suggest you spend your evening talking and joking with the bog-trotter, then leave him there, slumped across the kitchen table. (He'll be too drunk to mind.) Then go on upstairs and slip into your bunk with a Swede.

FRENCHMEN: The over-romanticized Gaul sounds great but looks terrible, scrawny, ferret-faced and constantly smoking his Gauloises. He seldom has the enthusiasm to do what he's supposed to be good at. But he has style, sophistication, and, boy, can he *cook*.

ENGLISHMAN: I thought London the reverse of Paris in that the food was lousy and the men delicious. Even the sixteen-year old Cockney shop boys have panache. (I do recommend the sixteen year old Cockney shop boys.) The limey tends to be winsomely reticent so *you* can have the fun of chasing *him*.

Caution: Do not beat your British boyfriend's bottom with a cane unless you have ascertained beforehand that he likes this. A few of them don't.

GREEKS: Everything you heard about Greeks is true. Back off.

JEWS: Full of doubts. He can think of twelve good reasons not to enjoy sex while engaged in it. But the typical Hebrew has had orthodontia, music lessons, and a graduate education. He should be a good provider and too insecure to cheat on you with any conviction.

BLACK MEN: There aren't enough of these to go around for the black women who want them and they should have first dibs.

SWISS: Genuine Swiss citizens don't emigrate and seldom leave Europe except on business. If a new acquaintance *claims* to be Swiss, demand to see his passport. He's probably a Greek. (See above.)

122

SCANDINAVIANS: Now, we're getting to the good stuff. The Norseman is not only tall, fair and gorgeous to look at, but he's a wholesome uninhibited lover as well. The Scandinavian is not likely to be rich, brilliant, witty, or sophisticated, but what's *important* after all?

If you live in a port town, you can heave on down to a Nordic seamen's bar and take your pick among the teen-aged deck boys. But remember that you are a lady. One at a time, please.

CHINESE: Some of them are bigger than they look, really. But if you do it with a Chinese guy, an hour later you will want to do it with him again.

ARABS: No matter how modern and liberal he seems over here, once back in his own country, he will revert to his patriarchal ways. If you split up, he will bring your children home to the Middle East "for a visit" and you will never see them again.

ITALIANS: An Italian man is not faithful to his wife. He isn't even faithful to his wife *and* his mistress. He wants romance more than an actual relationship.

LATINS: What you just read about Italians goes double for Latins.

Liabilities

Now that we have covered some of the possibles, let's rule out a few losers.

THE DRUNK: Revolting company after seven P.M., an unreliable provider, and you would be washing the bed sheets four mornings a week. If you're patient, though, you can pick up a little nest egg by insuring the swill pot down to his socks and pouring him all the hooch he wants. His liver will give out in a year. Ha ha!

(Most drunks and drug users believe they had a wonderful time while high. But was it *they* who had the good time or some alien presence made of drugs or alcohol that took over their brain and body? If they don't remember much of what happened, that supports the alien-presence theory.)

THE TRANSVESTITE: Forever depleting your cosmetics, splitting the shoulder seams of your best dresses, and stretching out your pantyhose. Yet he'll scream bloody murder if *you* wear one of *his* gowns.

THE WIFE BEATER: Even if you fancy yourself a masochist, you will soon tire of this brute. Bruises and abrasions tend to clash with your ensemble. Limbs work less well when broken. You'll have more scar tissue than a punch-drunk prizefighter, and permanent damage eventually results. Like deadness.

COUCH POTATO: If his favorite activity is slumping in front of the television, he'll be useless to fix things around the house.

THE GAMBLER: He can wipe you out in a weekend.

THE POUF: No matter how charming, the gay man is a bad bet for marriage. He will spend most nights out cruising and may come home, beaten up, several times a year. He may even bring his "new friends" home. These friends will usually be of a lower social caste, often freeloaders and thieves. And your husband's dearth of interest in your own charms will be demoralizing.

If a man tells you he's really bi-sexual, bail out; he's queer as a duck. Men who are actually bi-sexual identify themselves as straight.

MR. MACHO: That air of tough domination does not mean that Mr. Macho will take care of you but that he will make *you* take care of *him*. There is nothing fatherly or protective in his predilection for bossing women around. It's just plain exploitive. And there is no sign of love in unreasonable jealousy, either. That's only greed showing, and hunger for power.

GUY WHO BRINGS WOMEN HOME TO BOP THEM WHILE YOU WATCH.

GUY WHO DEMANDS THAT *YOU* BRING WOMEN HOME TO SO HE CAN BOP THEM WHILE YOU WATCH.

GUY WHO BRINGS *MEN* HOME TO BOP *YOU* WHILE

124

HE WATCHES.

(This last is especially tiresome because your lover won't show up with Matt Damon, but with Aaron-from-the-mail-room. Aaron-from-the-mail-room is a pock-marked nineteen year old who hasn't got his growth yet, and he keeps prattling about his Suzuki 350 as he's giving it to you while boyfriend abuses himself in the closet.)

BOOKWORM: The inveterate reader is wasting time better spent mowing the front lawn or re-plastering your shower. All he gains by this application is a head full of useless knowledge which he will employ to belittle you. (What? You didn't know Napoleon's second wife was a Habsburg? Stupid broad!.)

And the typical male bookworm is unacquainted with any practical skills, incapable even of changing a washer on your kitchen faucet. This nit must call an electrician when a fuse blows and will let you re-shingle the garage roof all by yourself while he peruses Dryden's Virgil.

LIAR: The classic case of a compulsive liar is Scott Peterson, a Fresno fertilizer salesman who told a cute young blond named Amber that he was a world traveler, calling her "from the Eiffel Tower" on New Year's Eve while he actually never left Southern California. He also mentioned that he was a widower. A few weeks later that became true and now Peterson is on Death Row for murdering his wife, Lacey. Pathological liars are evil and destructive in many ways.

SMOKESTACK: Do you fancy waking up every morning to the sound of twenty-minutes' coughing and gagging? How about stale tobacco fumes on your draperies, cigarette burns on your furniture, and a greatly-increased fire hazard? What's more, living with a smoker multiplies your own chance of getting lung cancer. One-third of the women who get it never, themselves, smoked.

THE FETISHIST: Some years ago, I was courted by a fascinating European named Alphonse and on the fourth date, I imparted the wonderful news that I was ready to go home with him. That's when he informed me that he believed the most erotic part of a woman's body to be the *feet*. I didn't think that a deal-breaker at the time.

"No problem. Mine are size *nine*. I'm *your* Dolly Parton!"

Well, he was happy about that. But I soon learned that Alphonse didn't want to play with my feet before intercourse or after intercourse or even *during* intercourse, but *instead* of intercourse. The relationship didn't last long. A girl likes to be made love to above the ankles once in a while.

THE AELUROPHOBE: The man with an unreasonable aversion to cats doesn't really like women either. He'll claim that he hates cats only because they're "too independent." But turtles are independent too, right? Does he hate turtles? Nuh uh. What really discomfits him about cats is that they're so manifestly effeminate and thus represent *women* who are independent. This man thinks cats and women should be humble, obedient, and submissive like dogs. Tabby wouldn't stoop so low and neither should you.

(You can make the complimentary assumption too. Women who hate dogs don't care for men. For dogs resemble men in many ways. You're forever cleaning up after the critters and they slobber all over you when you don't want them to. But, on the other hand, *dogs* are *worth* it.)

THE UGLY MAN: You assume that an ugly man will be so grateful to have gorgeous you that he will treat you like a princess. Sorry, no. He will probably be so insecure about the disparity of your attractiveness that he will be obtrusively jealous or try to undermine your self esteem.

THE LOSER: If anyone ever says, "My own family won't help me," run like a rabbit. There has to be a good reason his family won't help him. They know him better than you do.

Caution

THE WIDOWER: You don't have to rule him out. But before considering the tragically bereaved, find out what his wife died of and investigate thoroughly. If it was alcoholism or suicide, he may have contributed to it. Any condition that might have been aggravated by violence or neglect also gives pause. If the late Mrs. Him died of cervical cancer, he may be carrying the papilloma virus. Cut and run.

THE DAD:

"Hey, you want to watch my son pitch a Little League game?"

No, you don't, of course. Your suitor may hope to use you as a free co-babysitter, or just to get word back to his ex-wife that he's landed himself a great-looking woman.

A tactful refusal would be, "I think we had better see where the relationship is going before we bring the families into it."

Do *not* invest your affection in a boyfriend's children, no matter how adorable they are. That would make a break-up all the more difficult for them as well as for you. If you marry their father, there will be time enough to embrace them as members of your new family.

THE FRIEND: The caveat about getting involved with a friend is that you're too likely to suspend the wisdom you're learning here and *trust* the bum.

"But I've known Harold for *years*," you protest. "I'm *positive* that he wouldn't rip me off." Well, sister, perhaps you could count on Harold like a champ so long as you were only a friend. But once you demote yourself to lover, his former sense of honor and camaraderie no longer obtains. You may assume a new role as an adversary to be tricked and conquered.

To round out this chapter, here is a point system to help you make an informed choice of life mate.

1. He has a relative who is an auto mechanic. +10
2. He has a degree in engineering or accounting. +10
3. He has a degree in math or science. +5
4. English or philosophy. -10
5. His mother has a lot of money, marvelous taste in clothes and is your size. + 20
6. His father does the dishes. + 10

7. He plays the guitar. + 10
8. He plays the guitar extremely well. – 10
9. He plays the accordion. – 40
10. He doesn't eat breakfast in the morning. + 10
11. He drinks it. – 20
12. He has a subscription to the Wall Street Journal. + 10
13. To Popular Mechanics. + 20
14. To Hustler. – 40
15. Owns two suits. + 10
16. Owns three suits. + 15
17. A whole closet full. – 30
18. He's into running, boating, tennis. + 20
19. Bowling, pool. – 10
20. Video games. – 30
21. He belongs to Save The Whales, GreenPeace. +20
22. Masons, Knights of Columbus. – 20
23. K.K.K., Moral Majority. – 50
24. Drives a Rolls (his own). + 60
25. Someone else's. – 60
26. Watches Discovery Channel and BBC productions. +20
27. Documentaries and public affairs. +20
28. Food channel. + 10
29. Pay-per-view porn. – 40
30. Claims he doesn't watch TV. – 50
31. Has had a vasectomy. + 40
32. Has a charge account at: an art gallery: +20, a high end food store: +20, a liquor store –10, a pusher's: –20, a swingers' club: –100
33. Calls his mother more than once a week: – 20
34. Sees his mother more than twice a month: – 30
35. Lives with his mother: – 80
36. If a man makes the same income you do: + 5
Add a point for every $10,000 per annum he makes *above* your income.
37. If he can work with his hands and fix things around the

128

house. + 10
38. If he goes to church and so do you. + 5
39. If he goes to church and you don't. −10
40: He speaks a second language. +30
41. It's Klingon. − 50

Special Section: Macho Credentials.
Army 3
Navy 3
Marines 4
Coast Guard 3 (I used to give these guys a 1, till I saw them saving the lives of hundreds of my neighbors during Hurricane Katrina.)
National Guard (activated) 3
(Not activated) 0
Saw combat: + 3 for each tour
Busted down for beating up his drill sergeant + 6
Okay, now we're about to tote them up. If his score is:
Over 250: There is no such man. Go back and re-check your figures.
Over 150: Good enough. Grab him!
Over 50: Second-rate husband material. But a strong woman can handle him.
0: Most men are right about here.
− 100: A loser
− 200: Introduce him to your worst enemy.
− 300: You've got a hold of my ex-husband! Run like a rabbit!

Once you have evaluated a man on a practical basis and chosen him alone to serve you, it doesn't matter a bit whether your friends from high school think he's handsome enough, rich enough, or faddishly sharp enough. Just the fact that you have selected him gives your favored one enough status to hold his fat head up anywhere.

But I knaw'd a Quaaker feller As often 'as towd ma this:
"Doant thou marry for munny, but Goe wheer munny is!"
Alfred, Lord Tennyson

CHAPTER SIXTEEN: WEDDING FOR WEALTH

The Cinderella myth has probably contributed more to the oppression of western women than any piece of propaganda since the Bible itself. To refresh your recollection, this invidious tale is summarized below.

Once upon a time, there was this passive doormat of a girl named Ella whose step-mother and step-sisters stepped all over her. Forced to do all the drudge work in the house, Ella was so without resources that she spent all her free time spaced out in the fireplace. And so she was yclept "Cinderella".

Cinderella had two factors going for her, a pretty face (when the ashes were cleaned off) and small feet. (Size five or thereabouts.)

Even with these wonderful assets, she would have lived and died in that fireplace had her fairy godmother not decided to promote her. This fairy transformed the drab young woman into a glamorous one, as fairies do. Gave her a bath, put some highlights in her hair, and finessed her a designer gown accessorized with perfectly *divine* little glass slippers.

(Who would risk cutting their feet to bloody shreds by wearing *glass* slippers? The slippers may have been green, "verts", which was mistranslated as glass, "Verre".)

So Cinderella was whisked off to the royal ball where she connected with the crown prince of the realm. This prince was most probably a foot fetishist, for he didn't mind a bit that the girl's conversation was limited to remarks about ashes and chimney bricks, but really got off on her tiny tootsies. So when she bugged out of the joint at midnight, the prince picked up a slipper she had dropped and searched the kingdom until he found a foot small enough to fit it.

Then he married Cinderella and they lived happily ever after. That is, supposing the spoiled prince didn't grow up to be an abusive alcoholic or one of the more disagreeable kinds of pervert and if Cinderella wasn't flaked out by his obsessive attention to her feet and if the prince's royal relatives weren't too disgusted by his bride's low birth and lack of education and social graces.

The moral of this story is that a woman need be nothing more than passive, dainty, and beautiful to achieve that apex of feminine success, marriage to a rich and powerful man. Once this is accomplished, her fortune is made. She can shine in his light, hire servants to clean her chimneys, buy exquisite ball gowns, and brag her head off at high school reunions.

Seems so easy, doesn't it? Easier to pretty up and act dumb than to fight your way through some corporate hierarchy.

But hold in mind that there are millions of beautiful young women with all kinds of feet and a cursed scarcity of princes. Perhaps if you devote all your time and energy to "catching" a successful man, you can attain your goal. But if you put the same amount of work into becoming successful yourself, you will *surely* attain it. And you will be waiting on no one's pleasure.

Of all the women who dream of bettering their estate through a fortunate marriage, a pitiful few actually make it.

Because: Do you know whom rich men marry?

Rich *women!* That's whom.

What's more, men have more opportunities to, so are more likely to, marry above themselves than are women.

So the Cinderella myth doesn't offer any legitimate hope. But it does keep multitudes of underpaid secretaries from trying for managerial positions in the belief that they're only marking time until Prince Charming comes galloping through on his white charger to carry them off to a life of comfort.

The hoary adage that one who marries for money earns every penny is usually true. Rich men are used to getting every whim attended to, so they're even more tyrannical than their destitute counterparts. Would you be happy with the trappings of wealth if you had to sell your freedom for them?

When Gotrocks dictates that you be home by three o'clock every afternoon to prepare dinner, demands an hourly accounting of your time, orders you to give up your friends and inflicts his own menagerie of freaks on you, then imposes his gross and wheezing presence in your bed every night, you will be yearning for the good old days when you had little money and the priceless liberty to spend it, and yourself, wherever you liked. Rich husbands tend to remind you constantly that you are beholden to them for every morsel you eat and every stitch you wear. And they expect trembling, sucking, gratitude for every grudgingly-bestowed dollar, even though the time you put in as wife entitles you to an income as it would any other service provider.

Your rich husband may regard you alternately as a chattel or parasite according to his mood. Although your union was a stated or implicit bargain, the trade of your youth and beauty for his money, he will soon forget his end of it and become increasingly stingy as the marriage wears on. Until the simple monthly review of your expenditures abrades into a nightmare.

Some husbands are so stingy that they go over the credit card statement with a tooth pick, so you can't even get away with buying jewelry from the Home Shopping Network on the easy-payment plan. You have to counter by keeping track of everything he buys for himself. He probably spends more on beer than you do on jewelry.

Now with all these monitions, if you're still determined to have yourself a rich husband, make sure that's what you're actually getting. Some men have a rich fantasy life and that's all that's rich about them.

A beautiful ex-model I'll call "Pauline" met Wilfredo at a real estate class. He identified himself as a son of a fabulously-rich family of hoteliers, then declared that he loved Pauline and would buy her a little hotel of her own. She should have been suspicious when she Googled Wilfredo's name and nothing came up. Or when he wouldn't introduce her to any of those fantastically-wealthy relatives he supposedly had. Or when he promised to take her to the poshest ball of the year but – Oops! His son was just in an accident that rendered him brain-dead and he had to cancel. He was going to introduce her to his hotel-mogul father but – Oops! The old man just suffered a heart attack and he had to cancel. Wilfredo never even took Pauline to an expensive restaurant because he always just happened to have a yen for plain, ethnic food.

After weeks of dissembling, Wilfredo finally wrote Pauline a check for $800,000 to buy her hotel. It bounced like a wiffle ball but he couldn't be prosecuted for fraud because he hadn't received anything "of value" in exchange for his bogus check.

A German con man named Gerhartsreiter came to the U.S., erased his accent, and started calling himself "Clark Rockefeller". The surname alone was enough to snag him a brilliant Harvard Business School graduate named Sandra Boss. Ms. Boss must have noticed that her lover didn't have any valid ID, so couldn't get a driver's license, marry her legally, or even take a job. She supported him for years and let him take charge of her earnings. (No, I don't understand it either.) When she finally wised up, she had to pay him nearly a million dollars in a settlement. Now the phony "Rockefeller" is in prison for kidnaping Ms. Boss's daughter and is "a person of interest" in an old murder case.

An admirer who is hoping for a long-term relationship will tell the truth from the beginning, just as you do. But a predator won't scruple to award himself a degree from Johns Hopkins or Harvard Law. Then he'll tell you he's driving a cab for a living because "That whole other trip was so phony."

When a man sets out to sucker you by *pretending* he's rich, he's got one tremendous advantage. You feel that you have to pretend it doesn't *matter*.

"Ooh, darling. I don't care about your nasty old oil wells. All we need to be happy is each other and our love."

Phooey!

So you don't make him prove his claims of wealth and he can have you on indefinitely. You must assume a different stance from the beginning.

"You're rich? Oh, I'm fascinated! Now you can take me out to all the expensive restaurants I've been reading about. And then to your parents' estate to show me how the other half lives."

The phony will immediately counter that he doesn't care about "all that crap", meaning the accouterments of great wealth, which is why he chooses to dress out of J.C. Penney's and reside over a dry cleaner.

Get this, sister: a rich man may be frugal in some ways, like having the collar turned on his three-hundred dollar shirt, shutting off his phone service when he's wintering in Palm Beach, leaving his bowler hat in the Rolls so he doesn't have to pay to check it. And so on. But he does *not* live like a *poor* man. He doesn't buy Formica furniture or wear shirts of 100% virgin polyester or listen to a cheesy, down-market, stereo outfit.

The scion of a prosperous and patrician family can be spotted by the little details: alumni bulletins from Groton, a penchant for jumping horses, fluency in French, clothes that are very expensive but ten years old, his surname on a sky-scraper, and clues of a similar order.

You can not discern a man's income by his current lifestyle. That big car he drives could be borrowed, rented, or stolen. (The first time he leaves you alone in his car, look in the glove compartment "for a tissue" and check the name on the registration.)

He may own an impressive piece of real estate he bought with no money down, a piggy-back second mortgage and interest-only payments so he owes more on the property than it's actually worth. And he'll want you to bail him out of the deal with your life's savings.

Your high-flying suitor may be broke and living on credit while he hunts for a woman of means to support him. It's worth a bit of research to determine that the mansion, the limo, and the business are really his. Check his financial history to be sure he isn't some gambling entrepreneur of the "chicken one day, feathers the next" variety. These hustlers precipitously go bankrupt and expect their in-laws to support them while they talk up another big deal.

Get references. The same woman who wouldn't hire a cleaning service without checking it out with former customers and the Better Business Bureau is likely to elope with a man on a month's acquaintance, knowing only what he has chosen to tell. Her delusion being that any caution at all is unromantic and will jinx the marriage.

Baloney!

Check into your suitor's background before you get involved with him. Know where and what he comes from. The most important reference is the dreamboat's ex-wife or girlfriend. If he's a leech or a deadbeat or a bully, she'll tell you all about it. You must determine how many children he's responsible for and how he is meeting that responsibility.

There are a few ways to look him up. First Google the find along with the name of his industry. If you work for a retailer, you can call a credit bureau and get his rating. Look for angrily-worded bills in his mailbox, waste basket, desk, or on top of his refrigerator.

Meet his family first even if you have to fly to Tasmania. If Mom and Dad are dirt-poor, lover boy is probably living above his means. If they're rich, he's more likely to be frugal. If he declines to introduce you to them at all, he's either ashamed of them or ashamed of you.

Don't give your heart or anything else to a man until you

have established his bona fides.   He is to be considered broke, in debt, violent, syphilitic, and married until proven otherwise.

Moving On Up

The easiest way to get a rich husband is to be even richer yourself. You'll be running into candidates down at the yacht harbor and at country club affairs. Also, money attracts money. And most men will marry above themselves if they can.

But you should not give the impression of great wealth, especially if you have it. It would bring you more proposals than you can sort out, but most aspirants would be looking to better their estates.   Unlike *women* who marry for money, such men don't earn their keep by making a home.   Instead, they try to talk you into capitalizing their hare-brained ventures in the hope that they'll strike it rich some day and become independent of you.

A life-long swindler named Richard Bailey made his fortune wooing rich women and selling them worthless horses at astronomical prices. Most were too embarrassed to admit they had been duped and wouldn't press charges.   One victim he had left destitute quietly drank herself to death.   Another, the candy heiress, Helen Brach, wasn't so docile and began instigating prosecution. Bailey is now in prison for her murder.

So don't let a suitor sell you a horse or a franchise or anything else.

While keeping an eye out for the genuinely rich guy, you must work on yourself.   You should appear to be part of the class you aspire to join. Patronize the society hairdresser. Faddish cuts and artificial-looking dye jobs are a dead giveaway to humble origins.   And fashion extremes are out, along with cheap, synthetic fabrics.   Good enough for teen-aged fast food workers, not for future society duennas.

No matter how aristocratic you look, your voice can still give you away as Laverne or Shirley.   If you sound like a cigarette girl in a mafia nightery, take elocution lessons and mend

136

your grammar.

The catch here is that if your speech is dreadful, you probably don't know it.

Now for the hunt. You will not find the heir to fortune and title trying to fill a spare down at the bowling alley. It is necessary to betake yourself where the elite meet to schmooze. Join an Episcopal church in an upper-crust neighborhood. A sawbuck in the collection plate every week can put you in touch with the mothers and grandmothers of the most eligible bachelors around. Get on the boards of prestigious charities like museums and the heart fund. Join political campaigns for rich candidates. Answer phones at your public TV station.

Buy a dog and walk it through a ritzy neighborhood. Mutts are just as good as pets but not as props. So get a purebred at an animal shelter or breed rescue society. Hang out at horse shows and polo matches. Take riding lessons.

Get a job selling yachts, expensive cars, or mansions. Work for a society caterer.

Become a private duty nurse.

There is an entire industry devoted to serving the filthy rich. At this writing, you can spend thirteen thousand bucks on an eight-week course at The Starkey International Institute for Household Management, in Denver, and be on your way to a six-figure income as an executive butler for a dot-com tycoon or an estate manager for a superstar.

Once you have met and enthralled your aristocrat, it's vital to make a good impression on his family. They can make your life miserable and turn him against you. Be nice even if it means offering to help with the dishes, gushing over their obnoxious, aging Maltese, and showing up for Church every Sunday. If you can't get your prospective in-laws on your side, dump the guy and find someone whose family is more congenial. It's that important.

But for pity's sake, don't bring him home to meet your *own* family. Much as he may be smitten with you, he will not be ready for your senile mother's jabbering about soap opera characters. Nor will he admire your father whose pot belly can't be contained within his bowling shirt. Your sister who paints her toenails at the kitchen table and brags about the football players she's been gratifying in their campers won't entrance him either. Nor will your brother, the pot dealer.

So meet this catch in a presentable setting away from home. Explain that you love your family very much but they are too ill or too excitable to meet strangers. Or "If I introduce you, they'll want us to name the wedding date. They're so old-fashioned, poor dears."

If you live in a community-property state, get what you can from him in the form of gifts before the wedding. Then you may bring these things into the marriage as your separate property. And do *not* co-mingle your assets with his.

If you live in a title state, you must get as much as possible put in your name because the judge must award property to whoever's name is on it regardless of who paid for it.

All throughout your marriage, you must encourage large and frequent presents from your loving spouse. Jewelry is nice because it is considered your personal property at the time of the settlement. Don't pull so hard for clothes as they lose value quickly. So do cars depreciate unless they are classics. But make sure you get the titles in your name anyway. The only car you don't want is the one that has more payments due than it's worth.

During the post-honeymoon rapture, you should have a good accountant tracking down all your bashful groom's holdings. If he conceals capital and its income from you, you will not get your rightful share of the property accrued during the marriage.

(Also, if you sign a joint return with him, you will be liable for all the taxes on his income, reported and unreported, even if you never saw or knew about it.)

Unless you are at once hard-headed and well-informed, the old goat can slough you off with a piddling temporary alimony.

And you'll spend your sixtieth birthday selling underpants at Altman's.

The Pre-Nup

If you accept a man's proposal with the idea of marrying him for his money, make *darned* sure you're going to get some it. Many inept gold-diggers *think* they're marrying for money when all they actually wind up with will be fancy living arrangements on a short-term basis.

You may waste the next ten years caring for a sickly husband only to have him give his property to his children just before he dies or leave it to them in his will. You probably can't claim it as part of the community if he acquired his assets before your marriage.

We all know at least one poor fool who has signed away her marital rights in an air-tight prenuptial agreement and spends her humiliating days breaking her back to please her abusive master in the hope that he will die before he gets tired of her.

You need a prenuptial agreement to ensure your security. Laws vary from state to state so get a good matrimonial attorney to draw it up for you. She may suggest an irrevocable trust. You also should own a life insurance policy on him. You must pay the premiums yourself so the pay-out will go directly to you, not to his estate.

Most important: don't let your aspiring groom talk you into a "separate-estates" marriage. This sucker deal provides that should your marriage be terminated, each partner will take away only what he or she has brought into it. If he celebrated your wedding with ten million dollars in the bank and you with a dollar, sixty-seven, then after fifteen years of cohabitation, he gets to keep the ten million (with interest) and you get to keep the dollar, sixty-seven. (With interest.) If he made the money for the household while you raised the children, he gets to keep the money and you the children.

If a "separate-estates" marriage seems even halfway reasonable to you, consider that you can not take away with you the real assets you brought to the union, your youth and beauty. After a few years, you have depreciated like an old Honda Civic. Consider also that a marriage, of long or short duration, is a case of the wife's working for the husband. She runs his house, sees to his personal comfort, urges him to keep medical and dental appointments, and props up his ego so he is free to turn his energies to the furtherance of his own career. Seldom does a husband cook for, nurture, and wait on the wife.

And never does a rich husband.

The "separate-estates" contract guarantees that a man will have all the above-mentioned accommodations throughout the marriage for the mere cost of his wife's food and clothing.

In one notorious divorce case, the poor wife, Betty, signed a pre-nup agreeing that she would get nothing "if she refused to cohabit with her husband." Since the husband didn't want to turn over even the niggardly settlement the contract allowed, he abused her until she was forced to flee, than charged that she had "refused to cohabit" and he owed her nothing. The court ruled that he had driven her out. But even so, she didn't walk away with much. The provision that she could keep only her "personal effects" meant she owned nothing except what she could wear. The furniture, art work, appliances, silver, china, pots, pans, and even the cash in their joint account stayed with her ex. Betty was allowed to keep her clothes and jewelry. But since her ex was cheap, the clothes were ordinary and there wasn't much jewelry.

Here's another wrinkle: a man with children may ask you to sign away your dower rights, that is, waive your claim to the widow's portion of his estate as prescribed by the laws of your state, so his grubby kids can have it all. Do not!

Don't settle for a mere "life estate" or usufruct of your home unless his estate will provide for taxes and upkeep. A once-rich society friend of mine accepted as a divorce settlement, a "life estate" in her beautiful home on Sea Island. The agreement precluded her from leasing out the property and she had no income. So she sold her furniture, piece by piece, to make ends meet but eventually ran out of things to sell and could no longer buy food or pay the utility bills. Her electricity and water were turned off and she was sleeping on the floor in the cold and dark house and washing up at the nearest gas station. Country people who had once been her servants were kind enough to bring her food so she didn't starve. But she ultimately had to give up all rights to the house and, at the age of sixty-four, move to Manhattan to look for work. When I met her, she was living in a friend's walk-in closet on West 76th Street.

Don't sign *any* prenuptial agreement until your lawyer has assured that it compensates you for your time and services. And the diminution of your own market value.

It will be fairly easy for your suitor to talk you out of your marital rights if you have been insisting from the start that you only want him for his alluring self and have no thought of securing your own future. This you have been warned not to do.

"Marriage is like life in this – that it is a field of battle, and not a bed of roses." Robert Louis Stevenson

CHAPTER SEVENTEEN: ONCE HAPPILY MARRIED

Should you change your name? Certainly, if your groom's is much better than yours. If you're just a Jones or a Snyder and he's a Vanderbilt or a Rothschild, it's an instant upgrade in class. Also if your new career is just going to be as his help-meet, hostess, and stay-at-home mom you will be sharing his identity. But if you have a career of your own, keep your maiden name. Phyllis Diller, Angie Dickinson, and Raquel Welch were stuck for life with the surnames of long-discarded husbands because they began their careers under those monikers. And there were other already-established actresses who showed their love and commitment to new husbands by hyphenating their names. Farrah Fawcett-Majors, Patty Duke-Astin, Meredith Baxter-Birney, and Rebecca Romijn-Stamos all had to go un-hyphenate when the marriages fell apart.

Training

Decide first which of your husband's faults you can live with and which you won't tolerate. Then forget about the former. Don't even allude to them. And deal with the latter by absenting yourself from the man's company at the first hint of such misbehavior.

But don't nag.

When exercising day-to-day control over your mate, shrillness of voice should not be resorted to unless your intention is to repel the man. For that will be its effect. Hold down your rate of words per minute. As you speak more rapidly, your voice tends to rise in pitch until you're screeching like a train whistle.

If you make a habit of shouting at your husband, eventually his reaction will cease to be the appropriate groveling apology. For after just a few high-decibel sessions, he will learn to counter by slamming out of the house and careening off to the neighborhood bar where he will spend the evening and a good part of the grocery budget clearing his head of that godawful noise. When giving your husband to understand the deportment expected of him, you should *lower* your voice. A throaty near whisper is enough to strike fear into the heart of a man who reads its underlying threat: first that it's a preamble to the silent treatment, and, second, that the wrathful female party will not give any to the disobedient male party for a good, long time. Or until he has atoned elaborately for his transgression.

Control your voice and you will control the situation. This policy applies to most incidences of thoughtlessness and misbehavior on the part of your spouse.

An exception to this "cool rule" is an occasion of deliberate abuse by your husband. If, with malice aforethought, he actually sets out to hurt you, physically, emotionally, or financially, then it's time to erupt and breathe fire.

Understand I would never suggest that you, for example, wait until the miscreant passes out on the bed, then sew him up in the sheets so he can't move and beat him black and blue with a garden rake. (Use button and carpet thread.) But you must react appropriately. Taking cruel treatment with ladylike patience and resignation will not build good karma or get you an early release from purgatory. In fact, it profits you nothing whatever but only reinforces the aggressor's sadistic behavior, while you develop an ulcer or some other psychosomatic malady from choking back your bile. And you may be reduced to the infamy of taking out your frustration on your friends or your children.

So let your violent anger out where it belongs. In spades!

When a man deliberately hurts you, get loud, get litigious, get the cops!

Mind that, in some circumstances, you will have to delay the explosion and in others you must ignite it immediately. When you are among your own friends, family or co-workers, and husband Larry makes a maliciously humiliating remark, you hold your temper. Smile benignly and roll your eyes toward Heaven with a "Dearie, me. Here he goes again." look. And never seem to lose your good humor. Your associates will think the two of you just have a running joke.

When, on the other hand, Hubby makes those same unforgivable remarks in front of *his* friends, family, and co-workers, go right ahead and unleash your anger in all its dangerous fury.

"You think you can talk to me like that, you *&%#!!?" Call him something incestuous, then dump his dinner on his lap and storm out of the room,... building, ... maybe his life. You got so hurt and angry that you just couldn't help yourself.

If he comes back, he should be contrite and placating (with presents) and even better, he will have learned not to mess with you like that again. He won't realize that you would never pull the spitfire routine in the presence of anyone *you* care about. The average adult male would rather be impaled by the bulldog on a Mack truck than let his buddies see him shamed by a woman.

But do not dilute the effect of your righteous wrath by wasting it on misdemeanors. If hubby has a little too much to drink and makes a fool of himself at a party, just drive him home and forget it.

Arguments get bloody tedious when they are just rehashes of previous arguments. If you don't have anything new to nag him about then stow it.

If Hubby's offense is an on-going one, do not make your confrontation yet another rehash: "You never talk to me at parties." But state the specific instance. (Your "news hook.") "You didn't talk to me even once at the Foleys' party, this evening."

He knows he had better not counter with, "But I *never* talk to you at parties."

I used to consider infidelity to be merely a misdemeanor. But now with the likelihood of a cheater's bringing home a disease, even an incurable disease, even a fatal one, has made it much more serious. Another grave consequence could be making another woman pregnant which could break up your home or at least divert a good part of his time and finances away from you and your children

"Grit Your Teeth And Think Of England"

Should your husband pester you incessantly for sex, (The pig!) there aren't many tactful ways to avoid your conjugal duties. Claiming a headache doesn't fool anyone, and starting fights before bedtime can play Hell with your domestic tranquillity. And announcing that it's "one of those days" won't discourage most modern, healthy, men.

Some harried wives let their bodies go to flab and completely neglect their appearance which tactic may repel all but the most barbaric of husbands. But should you employ it, you will look lousy for *other* men too. An equally effective but immediately-reversible expedient is to do without bathing or changing your underwear. And maybe eat dinner without a fork, clip your toenails on the coffee table and use the toilet while he's trying to shave. Though men exercise such gross behavior themselves, they're horrified to see the like in a member of the superior gender.

The problem may be simply that you've been making sex too good for him. Try cutting down on the extra services. If you just lie back and snap your gum while he does all the work, the lazy bum's enthusiasm will abate. And insist that the television be placed where you can see it.

Suppose your loving spouse becomes one of those marathon copulaters, pounding away at you without surcease long after you're chafed and sore. First of all, don't let him stop in the middle for a breath, or for a chat. He's stalling. Keep moving, whether he likes it or not, and bring an end to the session.

Also, try a spermicidal foam instead of a condom and keep experimenting until you find one he is sensitive to. It will burn him. (Ha!)

Another way of dealing with excessive attentions is to introduce your hubby to a pastime that will channel his energies elsewhere. Make it something useful like leatherwork or refinishing furniture. Fishing can get him out of the house for entire weekends if you're lucky. Sailing is good if you can plead sea-sickness and stay home, but not if you will be impressed to scrape barnacles alongside him.

Don't push for tennis or running. Those sports are so healthful and energizing that they tend to *increase* one's sex drive.

What to do if your man is too affectionate? If Hubby wants to cuddle and grope and breathe on you without let-up when you would rather be left in peace, you can get him a puppy. Preferably one of the larger breeds. Dogs thrive on this sort of attention and he can manhandle a boxer all he likes.

Working

Should you work while married?

Only for yourself. Taking a job just to meet household expenses is a loser.

To illustrate this, we'll examine the typical evening at home chez your typical working couple.

At Six P.M., Mr. Him strolls into the apartment and turns on the tube.

At Six-thirty P.M., Mrs. Him rushes in, loaded down with groceries, bustles into the kitchen and starts dinner.

By eight, the dinner is over and the husband reads the paper while the wife clears the table and washes the dishes.

At eight-thirty, he watches football while she sorts the laundry.

At eleven P.M., husband looks over his baseball card collection while wife mops the floor.

And so it goes.

The miserable fact is that whether a wife has an outside job or not, nearly all of the housekeeping tasks will fall to her. So she will have two full-time jobs and only one salary. And the more money her husband makes, the more of her salary will be taxed away.

Even if you work forty hours a week, your husband will not respect your career as he does his own. Especially if you're not making as much as he is. Also, no matter how vital your paycheck is to the survival of the household, it will suit Hubby to think he's "man enough" to provide all the necessities, himself. So if you "choose" to work, it will only be to occupy your time or to buy yourself a few frivolous luxuries. Like a winter coat, or a refrigerator. But your little pastime must not be allowed to conflict with your "real" job which is taking care of the house and him. Just don't expect Hubby to come home from a hard day of earning the *real* money and help you out with *your* job.

A man's home is his castle. But his wife isn't the *queen*; she's the *staff*.

So forget about a bread and butter job. If Dreamboat can't support you adequately then what in blazes are you marrying him for? If he turns you on all that much, then just live with him until you have had your fill then move on to someone more profitable. You don't need a husband merely to sprawl in front of the set and holler orders.

But you *should* be working to further your *own* ambitions.

While your man is out rustling up the bacon, utilize your freedom from having to earn a living. Go back to college or grad school. Or take vocational courses to prepare for your golden future.

"Putting Hubby Through"

(Crazy if you do.)

Right this minute, countless thousands of naive women are

147

working overtime to support student husbands. They pay tuition, buy books, and feed fat faces in anticipation of some day assuming lofty new positions as wives of prosperous, professional men.

"I'll help him get his degree," the dreamer says. "Then he'll be bringing a lot of money into the house."

Sure he will, sister. But it won't be *your* house.

There was once a very common, but maybe precedent-setting, incidence of a woman who agreed to put her husband through law school on the understanding that he would reciprocate by putting her through medical school. So she made all the sacrifices necessary for her husband's career, as women will do. Then after becoming a lawyer, he reneged on his part of the bargain, as men will do. He walked out on the marriage.

("I'm being honest with you, Harriet. I just don't have the same feeling for you anymore. I need my space.")

The husband argued in court that he shouldn't have to pay alimony because his wife had been supporting herself adequately with clerical work. (And she has more to spend on herself now that the blood-sucker is gone.) But the judge ruled that the new lawyer would have to keep his promise to maintain his wife through medical school. "A degree for a degree."

The man's desertion was a matter of course. Just the fact that Harriet had lived with his old, unsuccessful, self meant that she wasn't good enough for the brand new professional. He wanted a woman he couldn't have hoped to win before.

When a man achieves a degree, or any other stepping-stone on his way to prosperity and prestige, he presumes that he deserves all the trappings appropriate to his new status: an apartment with a view, a BMW to replace his old Escort, Armani to replace The Gap, and younger, classier-looking women.

If you support your husband through college and graduate school, he will leave you further behind every year. (By his reckoning.) And you, slogging away at your bread and butter job, will fade into drabness.

Here's a better idea. Let your husband put *you* through college instead. Women almost never leave the men who have helped them move up in the world.

"I'm not pickin' up nobody's nothin'. Not anymore."
    Sally Field on her plans to enjoy domestic leisure in her middle-age.

Household Hints

However you decide to spend your days as a housewife, do *not* waste them actually keeping house. Housework is *not* good exercise; it's not aerobic. So there is no benefit to you besides the pleasant ambiance of a clean house.

Cleaning takes up time you could spend furthering your agenda. And what do you gain for your trouble? No appreciation from the other inhabitants, and the house will only get dirty again.

And men honestly don't value it, so why bother?

Man just home from work: "Did you pick up my shirts from the laundry?"

Woman, in jeans, covered with sweat and dust: "I was too busy cleaning today."

Man: "But I need my shirts."

Woman: "I vacuumed every room, dusted, washed, ironed and rehung the draperies, and scrubbed the bathrooms."

Man: "Can you run out and get the shirts now?"

You see? Men think housekeeping is something we women do for our own creative fulfillment and is of little benefit to them.

Husband to his bar buddy: "The joint is all upside down. My wife is scouring everything in sight. All I can smell is bleach."

Bar Buddy: "Wow, that's rough. You need a *beer*."

So don't clean anything until he complains about it. If he gripes that a certain window is so dirty that he can't see through it, then wash that window. The bottom part of that window. Change his sheets when he protests that they've become so slick that he's sliding out of bed and not until then.

And there is nothing remotely enriching about batting away dust which will just return tomorrow to be batted away again. Sure, you have to wash the dishes when you're out of clean ones and vacuum the rugs when you can no longer discern either the patterns or the colors.

(Nature abhors a vacuum and so do I. Most of those contraptions are so unwieldy that it's the equivalent of a day's work just pulling one out of the closet. So stash a light-weight electric broom type machine behind your couch and run it around when someone important is on the way over.)

Also, you must clean the undersides of toilet seats. (Sure, *you* don't see them, but...) It's inadvisable, though, to go to all the trouble of moving furniture just so you can scrub behind it, or dust the tops of picture frames and such unless your mother-in-law is very tall.

Things to say after "Excuse the mess".

"My nephew had his fraternity mixer here last night."

"The police are looking for the vandals."

"We're not allowed to disturb the crime scene."

"My son's film project requires a messy house. Go figure."

"Poor Mother was looking for her tiara again. Always forgets she sold it in nineteen-sixty-three."

"Did you feel that earthquake?"

If you clean your dwelling forty hours a week for the next five years, after a three-month lapse, it will be about as dirty as if you hadn't cleaned at all. So put those forty hours to better use. Attend casting calls. Learn to play the piano. Take up hat design. Then you will have something to show for your effort, someday.

And here's a handy little tip: If you have a friend or relative who is a compulsive housekeeper, stock up on cleaning products, invite her for a long weekend, and stay out of her way.

With any luck, she'll have the whole place sparkling by the time you wake up on Sunday afternoon.

Should your husband criticize the way you perform a certain housekeeping task, then respect his wishes and avoid performing that task ever again.

It is important to make clear before the marriage that, as a wife, you won't double as a maid. If your intended wants a charwoman, he can hire help or do the housework himself. (He's got bigger muscles than you and those biceps make for great scrubbing power.) He'll take your cleaning services for granted unless you set him straight at the beginning.

Should Hubby command you to make the house spotless for his mother's visit tomorrow, don't bother to retort that you're not his slave. (He's heard that a thousand times and still doesn't believe it.) But certainly do *not* knock yourself out actually trying to meet his outrageous demand, thinking perhaps that he'll be properly grateful afterward. Indeed, he will never repay you for your effort which only supports his conviction that he has a right to issue such orders.

So simply ignore his bellowing and do exactly as you like that day.

He will probably notice after a while that you haven't complied with his wishes. Should he have the nerve to bring it up, just shrug and say you didn't have time. And you may point out that the surest way *not* to get something done is to order you to do it.

So long as sex is better with you than he can get on the outside, (and this doesn't require that you perform any tricks; it's all in his attitude.) you don't have to be any good at anything else. He is sure to stick around no matter how lousy a wife you are in other respects.

While you're thrilling the guy in bed, it would make no sense at all to grovel about trying to be a good wife in the mundane areas.

The most useful advice heard in the military is "Never volunteer for anything." The same holds true for marriage. Your position should be that you don't know how to do anything. Replace a broken window pane? Goodness! You would *cut* yourself. Use the power mower? You don't have the strength to crank that nasty engine.

Your husband shouldn't think any the less of you for this manifest ignorance. He should expect it. Then he'll manfully take on these chores himself with a shake of his head and a "How would she ever make it without me?"

Some men have actually bragged of their women, "She's good for sex and nothing else." because that means they are successful enough to afford this luxury. Also that they are so very virile that they have to keep someone around for the sole purpose of dealing with their sexual needs. (Unless, maybe it's only *my* men who have bragged of that).

If, on the other hand, the sex is crummy or nonexistent, you had better be *great* at the other amenities.

Tip: If your husband asks, "Do you want to see my new truck-bed liner?" say, "Sure!" then put down the manuscript you're editing, walk outside, and look at his flipping truck-bed liner. And say something nice about it.

Tip: Let him watch his stupid westerns and sit there and "watch" with him. While Hubby's getting a charge out of drawled banter between "Doc" and "Festus", you can be reading a magazine or watching "House" and "30 Rock" at Hulu.com with earphones.

Sneaking Around

Just as passion is the worst reason to get married, the lack thereof is the stupidest reason for divorce. A marriage is a union of social and financial efficacy, not a romantic movie. And the most exciting and theatrical men usually make the worst husbands. So don't be lured away from a stable alliance by some heaving and rippling shadow in a distance.

Adultery is a sloppy course of behavior. It subjects you to all manner of embarrassments and diseases, cuts into your constructive time, and makes all your social relations ambiguous. It entangles you in a net of lies and deceits, ruins your reputation (if only among desk clerks) erodes your self-esteem, endangers your home life, and makes your mother carry on like a banshee.

What's more, adultery seldom offers the glamour and enchantment you enter it for. Most of your temptations to infidelity will be untempting. The kind of man who inhabits your fantasy world doesn't go sniffing around married women. And the man who does sniff usually has no interest in the woman herself. What he really craves is the titillation of cuckolding another man. (Letting someone else buy and pasture the cow while he gets the milk for free.) And the better the man he has stolen from, the more powerful he'll feel. So the reason for seducing another man's woman is not the woman but the man.

Also, the seducer need put out very little. The affair will have to be kept secret, so he needn't take you out shopping, or to elegant restaurants. You will be so busy with your home and family that you can meet Casanova only briefly, once or twice a week, have your physical encounter, then go your separate ways. This suits him just fine. You are as easy and casual as a prostitute but at no more cost than a motel room and an occasional drink.

You may be slyly propositioned by T.V. repairmen, window washers, and the fat guy who comes to the house to take baby pictures, all offering "the best time you ever had" or to "turn you every way but loose." And all thinking they're doing the bored and frustrated housewife a kindness.

Don't hesitate to advise them otherwise. At the first leering hint, mention that your husband is a Golden Gloves contender and president of the local shooters' club and on his way home for lunch. The would-be cuckolder should retreat to his stack of dirty magazines.

The aspiring seducer tries to insinuate himself into your affections by gushing that you're the prettiest, and most fascinating creature who ever chewed gum and finishing with, "I hope your old man knows how special you are."

Then you start thinking about the pot-bellied oaf, sprawled in his recliner night after night, swilling light beer and booing professional wrestlers, and say, "No, he *doesn't* appreciate how special I am. Why, he takes me for *granted*."

Sure, he does. But you take him for granted too. Forget it.

And don't imagine for a second that the heel trying to undermine your marriage would appreciate you either. He probably treats his own wife rotten. Or is too cheap or unbalanced even to *have* a wife.

Sure, you have marital problems like everyone else. But don't complain in detail to any man, except maybe your father or brother. Such revelations are always construed as a come-on. The sympathetic listener would commiserate with you for awhile, then declare that *he* would never treat a woman like that, especially one as awesome as you. And he just can't understand the oaf's behavior. Why, *he* feels like punching the bum *out*.

And then he would put his arm around you. And then... And then...

He's willing to issue a little flattery in exchange for your favors, but he won't pay your bills. He expects the "oaf" to do that.

Better to save your hoo-hah for the man who's feeding it.

So go ahead and tell your woman friends what kind of baboon your husband is, how you would walk out on the fat tub tomorrow if he weren't pulling down eighty grand per. You lose nothing by this exposé because all their husbands are baboons too.

As shabby as it is, though, adultery is preferable to divorce.

Should you get to pawing and panting over your immigrant gardener, you may feel compelled to meet him in the potting shed for some personal cultivation. But only an air head would walk out on her husband and family, file for divorce, split up all the marital property, drop a fortune on lawyers and then start all over again to assemble a new household with Guido. This too shall pass away.

And if you feel you absolutely must wallow in a tawdry extra-marital affair, at least be discreet about it. You owe this to your loved ones. Making it in your husband's bed is a "don't".

Join a health club, so that when you come home exhausted, glowing, and freshly showered, you can claim you had a heavy Pilates work-out.

Buy your husband the same brand of cologne your lover wears.

Have your affair with a man who has more to lose than you do if discovered. No penniless bachelors, please. A rich married man is safer. And there is always your parish priest.

Note: Just your being married doesn't mean you shouldn't expect and demand gifts from a lover. They're easily concealed. Have your secret admirer buy you a Versace, then tell your husband it's a forty-dollar number from Wal-Mart's. Rest assured he won't know the difference. Your lover can also give you jewelry for your safe deposit box, a house to be put in your mother's name, a car you can say you're renting, money you might have won at Bingo and more.

And thinking ahead, your husband may be inclined to forgive you a little dalliance if you end up with a pile of loot to show for it.

But never, *never* spend your husband's money on a lover. This would not only be more immoral than adultery itself, but it's stupid, destructive, and entirely unforgivable.

Like is attracted to like and class to class. So if you're really itching for a grand amour, propinquity dictates that you're liable to get a yen for your husband's best friend or your best friend's husband. Because, like Mount Everest, they're *there*.

You will have more opportunities to be together, but the situation presents a double-concealment problem. Two spouses to lie to instead of one. There will be several occasions for house-guesting with your secret lover and his wife, but extra caution is called for, especially with the temptation of nocturnal visits in the garage, behind the painting tarps, after lights out. The bathroom would be the safest amatory refuge because you can lock the door and run the shower. But if the deceived wife decides to wait outside for her husband to finish his nightly ablutions, that leaves you to bury yourself in the clothes hamper or attempt an escape via the laundry chute.

The embarrassment would be most acute if the two of you were discovered en flagrante. The old dodge of moaning out the names of your rightful spouses as though making an innocent mistake in the dark can be resorted to in a pinch, but it's never been known to work yet.

"Familiarity breeds contempt – and children." Mark Twain

CHAPTER EIGHTEEN: REPRODUCTION

The respective responsibilities of a wife, a mother, and a career woman are all difficult and time-consuming. You would be well-advised to choose only one of these callings if you want any time off for rest and recreation. Involve yourself in two of them and the recreation will be at a minimum. Take on all three and you will rob yourself of essential sleep, become subject to chronic stress, and get old before your time.

The arrival of a child into the household will plunge you into a smelly and hectic universe of diapers, two o'clock feedings, sleepless nights, measles, PTA meetings, back-to-school sales, perennially-running noses, and unbelievable income out-go. According to the US Department of Agriculture in 2005, it cost an average of $178,590 to feed, clothe, and school one middle-class kid up to the age of eighteen, not including college.

And you'll never get your investment back, either. Children have only a negative effect on your career, no matter what the career. And gratitude? There's no such thing. Solace and comfort in your old age? More likely, the ungrateful whelps will dump you in a state institution, have you declared senile, and confiscate your property.

Once you have given birth, your figure will never resile back to what it was. Your breasts will lose their firmness, even if you were nearly flat-chested to begin with and even if you don't nurse. The nipples will turn from pastel pink to rusty brown. Your breasts and belly will develop zebra stripes, red and etched in. (Go ahead and make with the cocoa butter until you glide like a snail. You can't prevent stretch marks.) And the only way to get rid of them is to have them sliced out with a scalpel.

Your belly will become pouchy. The hair on your legs will darken and grow coarse. So will facial hair.

These may seem trivial considerations. But you probably enjoy looking at your firm and youthful body in the mirror, more than you would contemplating some squalling, drooling, eight-month-old mound of quivering lard.

Not long ago, a national advice columnist took a poll among parents and more than seventy percent of respondents admitted that if they had it to do over again, they would remain childless.

"But children are a *blessing*" your Catholic Aunt Peggy insists.

No, they're not a blessing if you don't want them. Even *ice cream* isn't good if you don't *want* it.

Yes, it's selfish to eschew motherhood in favor of peace, prosperity, and convenience. But most children are brought into the world for selfish reasons too. The parents are deluded that the little rug-rats will actually bring love and joy into their lives. (Har!)

Another point: If you and your man don't love each other enough to make the commitment of marriage, don't create a baby together.

Every child has a right to the basic necessities of life. If you can't provide those, use birth control. (I wouldn't adopt a *puppy* if I couldn't give it everything it should have, and children are more important and more costly than puppies.)

As for the "noble" calling of raising children as a single parent, in my experience it takes all the resources of two intelligent, industrious, able-bodied, parents to provide one child with all the care it needs.

Paternity

Our problem is that women want babies, to hold them, nur-

158

ture them, love them, and raise the little creatures to be happy and productive citizens.

And men want babies too. To prove their virility, to enhance their status among other men, and to help them relive their own childhood. They also hope for vicarious success if the issue attains money and position beyond what they were able to achieve for themselves.

The fulfillment of the mother role will take up the greater part of a woman's time and attention for nearly two decades, until her youth has been entirely drained from her, in fact.

But most of the benefits of fatherhood are realized, or at least guaranteed, when the child is born. Which is why so many men don't stick around long after that.

The man in your life will probably push for a child early on. Sure, what risk does he take in paternity? In fact the less honorable he is, the less his potential loss. For his role in the project is brief, easy, and pleasant. Not for him the morning sickness, bloating, ruined figure, and torturing labor pains. Not for him either the lost sleep and nightly floor-walking when the little Martian gets colic or cuts a tooth. Nor the constant backaches from toting, bending and stooping.

If you have convinced yourself that personal contentment is found only in motherhood, and you can't be dissuaded from this folly, then at least prepare wisely. You will need a strong partner for this endeavor, so try to get one of the three or four men who would make good fathers.

A father must be a morning person, up at dawn to greet the day. If your swain sleeps till noon and stays out late, he is fit for adult company only.

Does your prospective husband like children? Note, the question is not *would* he like children. He has probably assured you that he craves a whole busload of the little droolers. But this ambition could have more to do with proving his fertility, passing on the family name, or spreading his seed over the earth than a genuine fondness for young people. You are planning the most important enterprise of your life and mustn't take any chances on the male half of the parenting team. Size him up by his behavior toward children *now*.

Does he spend time with his nieces and nephews? Play baseball with the neighbors' kids? Use a free afternoon to take fatherless youngsters to the zoo? Does he sometimes neglect you to work as a Big Brother, or on a Junior Achievement program? All of these are positive signs.

You may be thinking, "Clarence doesn't care much for other people's children, but he will be different with his own."

Don't go fooling yourself.

Sure, Daddy will proudly pass out cigars in the hospital waiting room, but he won't change diapers. He'll strut and glow when the guys tell him what a fine future defense back he's got there. But he won't follow the toddler around the living room, picking up everything it knocks down.

When the baby howls for attention, Daddy will be able to sleep through it. Or pretend not to hear. Or say, "I'm afraid I'll do something wrong. Here, *you* take him."

A husband gives his best energies to his career, and if there is any of him left over, his family may get it if they please him. Should he not enjoy the company at home and hearth, though, he will feel within his rights to spend his free hours at the club or the local barroom.

My friends, Sallie and Mark, seemed an ideal couple except that Mark wouldn't take on any parenting duties. Little Freddie and Gwennie had a sitter while Sallie was at work but the rest of the time, they were *her* problem. She never had time to herself to see a movie with her sister, or go shopping alone, or even take an uninterrupted nap. So she divorced Mark, giving him equal custody, and then he *had* to take his turn watching the kids. Sallie got her blessed free time.

No matter how many promises your light o' life makes when broaching the subject of an heir, turn him right off. Explain firmly that you are not about to spend ninety percent of your time mothering so he can spend ten percent of his father-

160

ing. And don't let him wear you down with cute baby pictures from Pampers ads. Your kid won't look like those.

A son (A man who sees progeny as an extension of his ego definitely wants a *son*.) will allow Daddy to recall briefly his own carefree youth. But after a short while, the male parent wearies of crawling around on the rug playing "big kid" to the offspring's "little kid". The pride of new fatherhood wilts quickly in an atmosphere of shrill baby demands and soiled diapers. The mutual gurgling and cooing soon gives way to, "Hey, Carol! Keep the baby in the kitchen with you! I'm tryna watch the *game*."

And so Mommy learns that this little animal, whom it took two to create, is hers alone to raise. This is true even if the father remains in the home. In the very likely event that he blows Diaperland for someplace cleaner and quieter she will have to support the child as well.

"He won't support his own children, but he takes care of the kids of that bitch he's living with now. I don't understand!"

Sorry, sister. Mother Nature has arranged it that way. Until very recently in human history, a male couldn't know which children were his own. He didn't even know he had anything to do with *making* children.

It didn't matter, either, because back in prehistoric times, children from the age of six on were actually assets. They could walk with the tribe and help gather food.

So the male had to take possession of and protect whichever children he found around him. In matrilineal societies, they would be his sister's issue. In modern, civilized, countries, they would be his step-children. For a father to desert his biological children is reprehensible, immoral, and illegal, but quite natural.

No matter how wonderful and paternal your man seems, don't even consider having a baby until you're fully prepared to raise and provide for it all by yourself. Because that's more than likely what you'll be doing eventually.

Child support is awarded to a mother in only about half the

divorce cases. And half of those men ordered to pay don't pay a cent. And the great majority of those who *do* pay don't come through with enough to keep the kid in sneakers.

To Be Or Not To Be A Cow

Nature has endowed us mammals with the lactary function because our young are born with undeveloped digestive tracts. Since they can not assimilate regular food, we manufacture adequate nourishment for them until their systems mature.

That is what your milk is for, to feed a baby that's too young to eat anything else. Get it? Nowadays, some very "natural" mothers don't understand this point at all, but think their milk is supposed to provide a major component of a kid's diet long after he can sit up at the dining room table and eat steak and potatoes with a knife and fork.

Should you have the poor judgement to bring a baby into this vale of tears, it's best to breast feed it for a few weeks to help your uterus pull back into shape. (It's good for the baby too.) Three or four months of nursing while the infant is being weaned onto Gerber's won't do you much harm. But if you let the little leech have at you much longer than that, you'll develop a dug line like some poor tribeswoman in National Geographic.

"But breast-feeding is the *natural* way," protests some latter-day flower child as her pre-schooler unbuttons her Indian cotton blouse for a snack. These persistent dairy queens are usually vegetarians (just like *real* cows) allow their hair to go gray and think any enhancement of their appearance to be "Really so superficial." They always look older than they are, after years of tending their soy crops out in the baking sun while toting the perennial nursling in a back pack.

Zero Population Replacement

It is this author's opinion that women in our country should unite in a birth strike. That is, refuse to have any more babies until the proper respect and appreciation are accorded this most

162

vital and difficult work.

Society's disinclination to value the nurturing function is manifest in its collective contempt for children (Evidenced by the under-financed and ever-deteriorating school system.) and for those women who devote their best years to raising them. There is no provision made for the day they will be out of a job, due to a husband's demise or desertion.

And full-time homemakers are more likely than any other group of workers to live out their senescence in unheated tenements, eating cat food.

When the powers-that-be in our society decide that motherhood is a primary and venerable contribution to humankind, it may do as other, more enlightened, cultures: make maternity expenses free or nearly so, give mothers an allowance for each child until it passes school age, provide good public schools and affordable day care. Our lawmakers are not going to make any such provisions so long as there is a surplus of babies. But let there come a shortage in the next generation of workers and taxpayers and the legislators may give motherhood some of the same support they give the defense industry.

My youngest sister who raised two handsome sons advises, "I wouldn't recommend having a baby to anyone who can be happy without a baby."

CHAPTER NINETEEN: SAVING YOUR MARRIAGE

The topic above is a lie because I'm really only interested in your saving *yourself*.

Let's face it; a good marriage is better than living single. (While, of course, a bad marriage is much worse.) It's most comforting to know that you will never again have to go out on a "first date".

Also, marriage is a small but significant defense against predators. When some nudnik makes a pitch for you, you can draw back in horror, thrust out your left mitt with its virtuously plain gold band and trill, "But I would never cheat on my wonderful husband." Even if he's not the least bit wonderful and you cheat on him all the time.

The putz who doesn't respect you as a human being, may respect you as some other putz's property and leave you alone.

If you have no children and no important investments together, go ahead and divorce to your heart's content. But if you are already a family, before you even consider divorce, sit down and do the simple arithmetic. From now on you will have to pay *two* rentals, *two* power bills, *two* water bills, *two* cable bills, *two* internet bills. There will have to be two sets of the child's furniture. If the children are the same sex, they can share a little room. Otherwise, the girl will be bunking in with you. Her clothes and belongings will be piled up in every corner of your boudoir. You can't even read in bed as you would keep her awake.

If your husband gives you his paycheck and doesn't abuse you, he's as good a husband as any. The concept that you deserve someone better, a devoted prince, is an illusion. Don't think there is some ideal lover out there for you: some handsome, wealthy, distinguished, dreamboat like the leading men on soap operas.

(Most of those classically-handsome actors on television

are gay as Christmas trees. And they're wearing make-up, hair-pieces, elevator shoes, and borrowed clothes, and reciting romantic lines somebody else, probably a woman, wrote for them.)

You should be aware that there are not any platoons of stunning men waiting for you outside in Cadillacs and your choice isn't between this jerk and George Clooney, but between this jerk and no jerk at all. So if you've got a good and gentle man who takes care of you, you're ahead of the game. Hold on to him. If you're determined to try for something better than you've got, stay married while you shop around for him. Just as it's easier to get a job when you already have one, being married could help your chances of catching another husband. For one thing, a married woman may have better entrees than a single one and your motives are less suspect. And being supported, you have more free time to go hunting.

And some men assume that if a woman is unattached, it's because no one wants her.

Cruising For Divorce

But naturally, if your man is abusing you, you're better off jerkless. When the marriage goes rotten, bail out ASAP.

For every day you stick with a brutal or sadistic husband, you will age four. The pernicious delusion that a woman's sacrificial posture will someday be rewarded is shared by battered wives everywhere. But get this; no matter how horribly a man abuses you, physically or emotionally, he will *never* be moved to make real reparations.

Many a broken and bleeding wife, having faith in the inevitability of justice, believes that if she bears with her husband's cruelty like the uncomplaining martyr of yore, he will, tomorrow or next week, stop drinking and totally reform. Suddenly smitten with a great infusion of virtue, he will devote the rest of his life to treating her like a queen to atone for all his atrocities.

This has never happened once in the history of the world.

You shall not ever, in this life or the next, be rewarded for unconstructive suffering. So do as little of it as you can manage.

If he ever *does* stop drinking, and reform, it will be for a new woman who demands the best from him, not for the kicked-around, worn-out victim.

Not only will you not be compensated for this monster's abuse, but instead you will wither under it, physically, mentally, and emotionally, until he's got you thinking you *deserve* periodic beatings.

Sure, after he's worked off some stress by batting you around, the abuser may try to placate you with a gift, but don't be placated. No man, and no make-up gift, is worth a lost tooth, a broken nose, or a permanently-injured back. Call the police and file a report.

By the way, when the police respond to a "domestic", they usually find the woman shrill and hysterical, while the man is calm, reasonable, and in full possession of his faculties. Gee, he sure doesn't look like a violent monster. Well, of course not; he just had his "fix". His tension has been relieved by beating her up. He's in a good mood now.

If alcohol was involved, it was the woman's own fault; she was drunk.

And the man couldn't help it; he was drunk.

If there are marks on you, you can have the creep hauled off the Central Lock-Up while you clear out the house and run.

To facilitate a quick escape from a violent man, it is necessary to have getaway money in your own name, in your own private account. You should also have a few traveler's checks tucked away in your Tampax box in case you have to run for your life at two in the morning.

It won't do to sit up in a bus shelter all night until your bank opens at ten AM.

166

CHAPTER TWENTY: PREPARING FOR DIVORCE

When Things Go Terribly Wrong

You have to take measures at the first hint your husband is no longer thrilled with you. Be alert for signs that your marriage is falling apart. If home is no longer his favorite place to be and you and your children are not the people he chooses to be with. If he parties away money that should go for household expenses. If he wastes time and capital on computer porn or phone sex.

If he cheats on you, that's a good indication that he doesn't care anymore. If he uses a phone and doesn't let you see the bill, there's a good reason. Her name is probably "Amber".

The only way to guarantee a comfortable divorce is to prepare for it while you're still blissfully married. Once a husband turns bad (Which can happen very quickly if he loses his job or gets you pregnant.) the assets will disappear from your joint account and your safe deposit box, the household cash will dry up, and you'll find yourself shaking the couch cushions for bus fare. So get those extra dollars out of him while you're still his little darling and stash them.

If this careful provision for your future seems a bit cold-blooded, be advised that nobody is more unfeeling, or has less conscience, than a man who no longer wants his woman. Ask any divorcee.

(Note: You get a vested interest in your husband's social security after ten years of marriage. So if you put up with the creep for nearly that long already, hold off getting the final decree until your ten years have passed.)

We hope that your preparations are never needed and your husband remains happily devoted to you for the rest of his days. Even so, a cache of getaway money will afford you the confidence that you stay with him because you want to, and not because you would starve on your own.

Take Precautions

Write down his social security and drivers license numbers and also make a list of all bank accounts, brokerage accounts, and financial instruments. If he stopped loving you a long time ago, he may have been spiriting away his separate or joint assets all along in anticipation of a getaway. I know it's a nuisance, but you must review all financial statements every month. Do *not* let them be sent to his office.

You have to change your password, close your e-mail account and open a new one so he can't hack into it. You may have to erase your whole hard drive or just junk the computer and start fresh.

After walking out on you, the prodigal husband may come crawling back, proclaiming that he'll make it all up to you if you will just stop the divorce proceedings. What he really wants to do is buy time. He's got to keep your lawyer from putting a freeze on joint assets and getting an accounting. He'll act very loving if he has to, while quietly looting the brokerage accounts, re-mortgaging the house and hiding the money, selling out his business and emptying your safe deposit box.

Here's another nasty trick: your estranged will call the utility company to say he has moved out and ask them to turn off the gas and electric and refund his deposit. He'll do this on a Friday evening, so you and the children will be in the cold and dark at least over the weekend. Rather than freeze, you will pick up the children and go to your mother's. While you're at your mother's, your scumbag ex and his brother, Ritchie, will enter your house and take out everything of value: the appliances, all the furniture that's worth anything, and even your jewelry which he will pawn or give to his new girlfriend.

You won't have a criminal case against him since, legally, your husband has as much right to the property as you have. So you have to hire a lawyer and fight him in court for your own belongings. For years.

In the rare event that he is fair with you, be nice and let him have the humongous, large-screen, high def, TV. Come on; be cool. You know very well that you can be just as happy watching "Desperate Housewives" on a smaller set. Once he's ensconced in his recliner with his over-size TV, he shouldn't object to your taking the bedroom suite and dining room set. Also give him his tools and anything else that goes with his hobbies and pastimes. He can give you the equivalent value in something else. If he really, truly, wants the dog or cat, give him the flipping dog or cat. Anything bought for the children goes with the children. The play station is little Brad's. It's not yours and not his father's.

Getting Back Into The Game

Okay, so your husband left you for a younger woman. His loss.

First you will lose weight. You won't have to work at this; due to the stress of all the changes in your life, it will just drop off. Then you will change your hair. Curl it, dye it. Buy some new clothes to show off your new figure or borrow your daughter's.

After a divorce, who gets custody of the friends? If your ex is rich and powerful and you were nothing but his "helpmeet", then most of the crowd will go with him. If you were the one with all the charm and style, a sought-after hostess, you will still be in demand.

Placing The Little Darlings

If you have children, now you are faced with supporting them on a meager "female's" salary with no father. So, don't. Let Daddy have custody.

Your falsely-sentimental ex will not admit that he doesn't want the little chips off his old block. In fact, he'll probably sue for their custody in an effort to unnerve you so you will settle for less than your fair share of the property. So just surrender immediately and stick the varmints on him before he has a chance to change his tack.

Before you shriek in horror at the very idea, here follow some unassailable reasons:

1. You can't stay home with the little wet-noses anyhow. You will need a full-time job just to put food on the table. So they will be spending most of their waking hours in daycare, regardless.

2. Men make a lot more money than women do, and Daddy can give your darlings a higher standard of living than you can, including a better class of day care.

3. It's easier for a man with children to find a wife than it is for a woman with children to find a husband. Inbred maternal instinct compels females to dote on little beasts that aren't their own. But men are less inclined to support "some other guy's brats." Especially if the children are male and replicas of their non-supporting biological fathers.

4. Your schedule is going to be hectic: boning up for your new career, adjusting to the single lifestyle, and getting yourself back into circulation.

"But I'd never give up my child!" you declare hotly, clutching little Biffie to your bathrobe.

Think again. If you can't imagine sleeping late on weekends, reading or watching TV without interruption, or spending most of your paycheck on yourself (Even after the deduction for child support.) consider that you would get to be the "fun" parent, the one who goes to the zoo on Sundays and buys ice cream, while your ex will be stuck as the custodial parent who has to pick up laundry and nag about homework.

Otherwise, you could devote your next twenty years and the better part of your income to an enterprise, the end product of which will be (at best) a very ordinary person.

So much for motherhood.

If you have been a good wife, the clown who deserted you is likely to realize his mistake, discard the bimbo he ran off

170

with, and try to come back. He may even offer to restore whatever is left of the property he stole on his way out. You may act forgiving just long enough to get your entertainment center back. But don't really fall for him again.

As Phyllis Diller said, "Remarrying your ex-husband is like having your appendix put back *in*."

CHAPTER TWENTY-ONE: JUST BUSINESS

When You Work For A Man.

Do *not* let your male employer presume a friendship. You are in his life for one reason: to make money. If you let him think you're friends, he will use that "friendship" against you. He may try to get work out of you on the basis of your "friendship" rather than your financial association.

EMPLOYER: "Say, Trudy, dear, would you mind picking up my dry cleaning on your lunch hour?"

YOU: "I'm sorry, Scott. I won't have time during my lunch hour. But I'll be happy to run your errand now, if someone else will take over this typing."

Make it clear that you're at his beck and call, but *only* within the parameters of your employment and when he is paying for your time.

Take your break exactly when told to. If you stay at your work for five more minutes just to finish up what you're doing, you may not take that extra five minutes at the end of the break. You would be accused of goofing off.

Suppose the boss gets drunk and, blubbering with self-pity, invites you to stay overtime and keep him company while he sobs about his bitchy ex-wife or ungrateful children.

BOSS: "Whyancha schtopp an' have a drink wi' me. I gotta talk to some'un."

YOU: "I wish I could, Scott, but I have to rush home to my family. Would you like me to call someone for you?"

You have nothing to gain by hanging around to commiserate with him. No matter how sloppily grateful he acts at the time, this precipitous bonding will not make you his equal. He will not give you a raise or a bonus for listening to his woes. In fact, once he sobers up, he's likely to be ashamed that you saw him looking foolish and find an excuse to fire you.

When A Man Works For You

Don't strive to prove how democratic you are by treating your male employees as friends. They may well use the friendship against you by leaving work early, coming in late, and taking overlong lunch hours (with the most worthy of excuses, of course) or by asking for advances on salary. Hey, you can't fire your good friend just because he dropped your favorite vase or botched an order and cost your company a valuable account.

If you hire someone to perform a service: paint your fence, put in shrubbery, DJ at your daughter's quince or some such, specify in writing that he himself will do the work according to the contract or he might send you his mutant nephew, Jethro, who never does anything right.

Check any contractor's references and reputation with the Better Business Bureau. When having any work done, you must write "Time is of the essence" on the contract and delineate financial penalties for every week the contractor goes past the deadline. Do not pay in advance.

You should not, ever, leave a workman alone in your house. If somehow it becomes vitally necessary to do so, put the remote in your pocket before you leave, so he doesn't spend your absence watching pay-per-view porn on your cable.

If you have to go by yourself to get the car serviced or repaired, you can use the man in your life as a reference. "My husband said to come here for the repair." (Or brother or father or boss.)

If you employ an attorney, understand that even your phone calls will be billed for his time in seven-and-a-half-minute increments. If you go to visit him at his office, his secretary will make a note of the time you entered and the meter will be ticking away until you leave, even if you spend most of the time listening to him brag about his golf game.

What I Learned From Court Shows

Never give anyone a cell phone unless, maybe, it's the pre-paid kind. A talkative boyfriend can run up four-figure toll costs in a month, before you get the bill. There are plans that allow for unlimited use, but it seems some poor fools don't know about those.

Don't accept collect calls from inmates unless they're first-degree relatives and they committed their crimes on your behalf.

Never have a joint bank or credit card account with someone you're not married to.

Never co-sign for a purchase for someone whose credit isn't good enough to buy it himself.

Don't make bail for anyone but the family breadwinner. No matter how the inmate cries and begs for help on the phone, once he breathes the free air, he will declare that he never *asked* to be bailed out, your contribution was a gift, and there was no plan to repay you. If you feel compelled to get anyone out on bond, drag the person to the bail bondsman's office and have him sign a handwritten IOU for the money with the repayment plan delineated, including a provision for interest at the highest legal rate if the payments aren't made timely. And get the title to his car for collateral.

Should you lend a man money, when it comes time to repay, he'll claim it was a "gift", and that you were trying to "buy his love".

Never lend any more than you can afford to lose. And write "Loan" on the back of the check so the borrower has to write his endorsement directly under it. A promissory note doesn't have to be notarized but the repayment plan must be stated using calendar dates. "When the debtor gets his settlement/ tax refund/ job..." etc. won't do for a repayment date. Because if he never gets the promised settlement, tax refund, or job then he won't owe you anything, ever.

174

"A witty woman is a treasure. A witty beauty is a power."
George Meredith

CHAPTER TWENTY-TWO: BEAUTY: DO WE NEED IT? CAN WE HAVE IT?

Healthy Narcissism

During a couple's first assignation, the man will usually strut around naked, un-self-consciously displaying bird legs, pot belly, and sundry scrotal ruptures as if he were the stuff dreams are made of. While any woman who doesn't resemble a Hawaiian Tropic ad will timidly hide her negligible imperfections under a sheet.

The incongruity here is that a woman, with her romantic notions, is more likely to be grossed out by her date's deformities. (Unless she is already hung up on the toad before he takes his clothes off, in which case she will decide they're "cute". It's sad that few women wait that long before consummation anymore.)

The man may have no romantic notions at all. Sometimes he is interested in immediate release and doesn't care if the woman who facilitates it is a "Ten" or a "One". He is so eager to get in the midst of things (in a manner of speaking) that he won't stop to take an inventory of sagging breasts, stretch marks and cellulite.

Sad to say, a male doesn't require the remotest attraction for a female to use her as a surrogate for Charlize Theron. But if he doesn't love the woman he is with, he will start finding fault once the conquest is made and the thrill has worn off.

If you don't accept yourself, it's possible that no one else will either. So love yourself with all your heart, no matter what you look like. Any part of your body that's skinny is "firm and girlish". The fat portions are to be considered "full and voluptuous". Remember this attitude and live by it.

NOTE: You only have to be pretty enough to get one date with a man. After that, it's your personality and accomplishments, the goods beneath the wrapping, that count.

First, you must decide how to deal with major flaws in your physiognomy.

Perfect symmetry does not make a famous beauty. Jackie's wide, wide set eyes, Sophia's buxomness, Audrey's gaunt thinness, and Julia's over-generous mouth are what make those glamorous ladies unforgettable.

Let's take teeth as common irregularity. Should you have a startling malocclusion (can eat oranges through a tennis racket) do not conduct conversations with your hands in front of your mouth. Any self-conscious camouflaging gesture looks worse than the flaw it's contrived to conceal. And don't refrain from smiling either. A smile makes you look younger, prettier, and more personable. These advantages far out-weigh the demerit of crooked teeth.

If you're miserable about your over-bite, it's never too late to start orthodontia which can be invisible nowadays as well as affordable on a payment plan.

The same policy is to be followed for any distinctive feature. Either change it or flaunt it.

If you are afflicted with some gross physical deformity, new acquaintances will see that and nothing else for the first three and a half to six minutes after your introduction. Beyond that, the force of your personality will become the most interesting thing about you.

The principal advantage of being pretty is that it frees you from the anxiety of wishing you weren't ugly.

Beauty also gives you the confidence to sail into a roomful of strangers with a toss of the locks and a flash of the teeth, knowing you will be accepted, even admired, with nary a calorie of effort on your part. But if that's all you have to offer, you will be obsolete within a year. Understand that beauty is useful only up to a point, beyond which it becomes a gift to the beholder but a burden to its possessor.

Sometimes, a spectacular face and figure overwhelm the poor creature inside them. A woman who has made capital of her looks most of her life may feel worthless when they begin to fade.

What types of men chase tall, skinny, models? Mostly those who seek trophies. Fashionable looks attract the jade who will throw aside today's arm-piece for the younger, fresher, item he meets tomorrow. And the reprobate who refuses to see anything of value beneath the shining hair and flawless complexion. It's all about conquest and variety.

In modern times, countless men have been ruined by pornography. Lusting obsessively after young, beautiful, silicone-enhanced, models, they can no longer enjoy normal intercourse with a normal woman. They think their sex partners should look like the expertly-coifed and cosmetized girls on their sex videos and feel cheated if she doesn't. She should behave like them too, displaying herself for his delectation.

Get this: the man who loves you for your fabulous face and enhanced figure does not love *you*. Any more than the man who loves you for your rent-controlled apartment or your grandpa's hat factory.

The "ravisante" is more likely to be exploited than her less-favored sisters. Not only is she a more visible target for the wrong sort of man, but she is more susceptible to their deceits as well. It happens that a woman will do almost anything for a man if she believes he loves her. And the beauty is more prone to believe this easy lie than most. She has fallen prey to the myth that men are enthralled by the mere sight of her. (Isn't that what the commercials tell us? "Be beautiful and he'll love you."?) The world is supposed to be a rich and benevolent place for her. But by the time she realizes the applications and limitations of her special advantage, it is usually too late to make the most of it.

Wise up before you wrinkle up!

A man does not feel an irresistible urge to give his life over to someone merely because she's dishy. He may want to climb her tree just for the glory of having been there. Or he may want to be seen with her. But love doesn't enter into it.

Additional warning: It's the ugliest men who try to make a beautiful woman feel insecure about her looks: "You've gained some weight since the last time I saw you." or "You're looking tired."

They try to break down your self-esteem, so you will think, "Gee, he's right. I'm not perfect. Maybe I don't deserve better than this fat, old man."

Handsome men don't feel they have to prove anything.

The Dangerous Barbie Doll Fantasy

In the early fifties, every little girl wanted a "Ginny Doll". The hard plastic Ginny, made by Vogue Dolls, was eight inches tall and looked like a four-year-old girl. She came with a wardrobe trunk and there were more dresses you could buy for her if you had a mind to. Through the years, accessories, furniture, settings, and even a dog were manufactured for Ginny.

In 1953, Disney brought out the film, "Peter Pan", and followed up with a "Tinkerbell" doll. The famous pixie was vinyl, about twenty inches long, and looked like a fifteen-year-old girl. Tink had her trademark blond topknot, elfin face with a ski-jump nose, a bosom, a small waist, and long, shapely legs. Later, in 1959, Mattel brought out the classic Barbie doll. She was pretty much the Tinkerbell doll in hard plastic, shrunk down to eleven and a half inches, with the same blond topknot, ski-jump nose, curving bosom, small waist, and long, shapely legs. But she had the Ginny doll's wardrobe and accessories.

While the original idea of a doll was that it represent a baby to be nurtured, Barbie looked like a little girl's vision of herself as she hoped to be in ten years. But that was a hopeless dream. For if Barbie were enlarged to the size of an actual woman, say

178

five-feet, six-inches tall, her measurements would be thirty-two, nineteen, twenty-nine. Do you know any real person that slender and curvaceous? Neither do I. Neither does anyone. Even Playboy Magazine, which pays the top fees in the world for figure models, has never encountered a lady with those dimensions. But still, girls try to approximate the doll's fantasy image by starving themselves into sticks then adding breast implants. The poor things are then too malnourished to grow long Barbie hair, so they get extensions. They get their teeth capped to show an unnaturally white smile. They can't find straight men who are as handsome as the "Ken" doll so they hang out with gay guys in an effort to complete the perfect picture.

Adding to the problem is the fact that some men who can't relate to real women think they have a right to a partner who *looks* like Barbie.

Perhaps the media are to blame. In Hollywood films, almost all the female characters just happen to be young and beautiful, even a waitress in a diner or a toll bridge worker. An unsophisticated male gets the idea that gorgeous, sexy, women are just everywhere, so how come he doesn't have even *one*? Even on family sitcoms, the "husbands" tend to be silly-looking, fat or wimpy schlubs while their "wives" are slender and beautiful.

(That juxtaposition originated in burlesque when a baggy-pants comic did his shtick using a beautiful showgirl as a foil, then started on TV in 1949 with pudgy, bug-eyed, Jackie Gleason in "The Life Of Riley" opposite the lovely Rosemary De-Camp. The William Bendix version of "Riley" came later, in 1953, with the same format.)

Living Plump and Loving It

I just saw a TV commercial for a diet nutrition plan. The spokes-model pranced around with a dazzling smile while "Size Ten" flashed on the screen.

"Well, good for her," I thought. "She got herself down to a

size ten."

But, no-ooo! It quickly transpired that the size ten was where the model had *started* and now she was proudly down to a size *four*. That was the achievement she was so giddy about. Ten would have been a fine size for the girl, but now her figure looked like an arrangement of knitting needles.

Keep in mind that a normal female is supposed to be twenty to twenty-five percent fat. It makes no sense to strive for the translucent thinness of a fashion model unless you model fashions for a living. Take pride in your curves. Your ideal weight from the male point of view, is probably ten or twenty pounds heavier than as you perceive it.

An easy way of telling is that your waist measurement should be no more than half your height. If you're five-foot, four (sixty-four inches tall) your waistline should be no more than thirty-two inches. But I don't know if you're allowed to pull your stomach in. I always do.

If you're at the upper-limit of your healthy weight range, just maintain that. Should you go on a stringent diet to try to be fashionably skinny, you are most likely to teach your metabolism to live on less. Then when you go back to eating normally, you will regain more weight than you had lost and end up heavier. (They call it "yo-yo dieting".)

(When I realized I would have to cut my food intake by about one-third for the rest of my life just to keep off that last fifteen pounds, I decided I'd rather be a little plump. Who says beautiful women all have to be the same size?)

Though some men marry thin women to conform to peer pressure and the mode of the day, they often lose interest in the beanstalks and wish they were wallowing in a mountain of soft flesh somewhere.

And as for women, those poor gaunt souls on perennial diets often envy the zaftig woman her independence of conventional standards and all the good meals she must be enjoying. (I know I used to.)

Should you choose a life of complacent corpulence, you

must learn to make your own clothes because really elegant frocks in larger sizes cost the world. So pick up the most beautiful fabrics available and designs with vertical seams. Your styles and colors can be superlative even if your figure isn't. And it's necessary to take more pains with your hair and make-up than your skinny friends do. Your soigné, impeccably-attired, impression will be one of enormous glamour. If you believe you're beautiful in spite of, or because of, your tonnage, others could be psyched into believing it too.

The very worst you can do is decide you're a hopeless slob and treat your body like a cumbersome abomination.

When you have to look thinner temporarily for a photo session or a beauty contest, drink a lot of prune juice and lemon and water. (A diuretic) Avoid salt and other liquids containing sodium, including diet soda, so as not to get bloated. And eat sparingly. Some professional beauties go to the extreme of laxatives and enemas. Don't you! Instead, take one chromium picolinate pill every day. It helps metabolize sugar.

To look your best for a lover, realize that you're probably lumpy at night, swollen up with everything eaten and drunk during the day. So be a bit "modest" at bed time, showing only parts of the body at a time in teasing flashes.

In the morning, you will be dehydrated and thinner. So that's the time to saunter around naked, showing it all off.

Above all, don't call a man's attention to imperfections in your figure as he may not notice them himself, especially when you're naked. If he's a healthy guy, he should be slobbering down his chin at the very sight of you.

Most men wouldn't even *know* about cellulite if we didn't tell them, so don't you be fool enough to tell them.

Really Fat?

Are you exceedingly fat? No, if you're simply too heavy to star in a soap opera. Yes, if your doctor advises that you're endangering your heart, health, and life expectancy. No one else's

181

opinion matters. Not even your own, as you may have body dismorphia and think you're too heavy when you're a stick. What are your alternatives if you are truly obese? You can join proven support groups like Take Off Pounds Sensibly (T.O.P.S.) Over-Eaters Anonymous, and Weight Watchers.

Often a woman can acquire the figure she wants by relocating to a healthier mode of life. My best friend from High School, "Naomi", was beautiful, talented and loveable but simply too heavy as a teenager. She didn't have the choice of boyfriends she deserved, was always under pressure (especially from her mom) to lose weight, so was forever dieting. After college, Naomi moved from Northern New Jersey to Amsterdam and adopted the healthful lifestyle of her new city. Home in suburban Jersey, she would have had to drive everywhere. In Amsterdam, she doesn't even have a car but travels by foot or bicycle. She lost the extra weight, pursues her profession, and has been happily married to a Dutchman for many years. She and her husband take their vacations as walking tours through Europe and Asia.

Yes, changing your geographical location can change your figure. Hey, join the Peace Corps. That will knock it off you. Or just move into a five-floor walk-up over a Chinese restaurant.

"Meal Options"

Note: I personally find that when I have a big breakfast, my stomach stretches so that I'm hungry all day. So if I get a hankering for a great breakfast: two eggs over-easy and buttered whole wheat toast, I have it at dinner time, *instead* of dinner.

Keep a food diary. For example: "Ten A.M: Half-cup of cereal with low-fat milk: 180 calories." It's easy these days because the food packages in your kitchen now list calorie counts per serving. If you eat at fast-food stands, you can go on-line for the nutritional information on every item they sell. I guarantee you will lose weight because you will be ashamed to tell your food diary you had a Snickers bar at midnight.

There is a *right* time to eat that Snickers bar, which is just before beginning a tennis game or some other form of exercise. Don't eat a dessert if your next scheduled activity is sedentary.

Craving a particular food does *not* mean your body should actually *have* that food. Often people crave food they're allergic to. If you get a yen for something unhealthy, wait ten minutes. It will probably dissipate. If the craving doesn't go away, bargain yourself down. Should you get a yen for chocolate cake, maybe you can settle for a scoop of chocolate ice cream which has more nutrition and fewer calories. Maybe even a glass of chocolate milk.

Do drink milk with your meal just as you did when you were a kid. Milk does not make you fat. It clears the palate between bites and makes the meal more satisfying so you eat less.

I drink more milk than a calf and it doesn't make me fat. You get a *discount* on the calories you take in from milk. I *mean* it. I don't believe it's a sin to have a piece of chocolate if you accompany it with a glass of milk.

When you feel a yen for apple pie, start with a baking apple, core, peel, cut it up, and bake it in the microwave. (I use the "fresh vegetables" setting.) When it's done, sprinkle with cinnamon and a yellow packet of sweetener. You get a delicious, hot, fruit dessert for the calorie count of a plain apple. Another rich, low-calorie dessert is fruit cocktail packed in it's own juice, topped with an aerosol whipped cream.

You can also make a modified "chocolate egg cream." Mix four teaspoons of Walden Farms Calorie-Free Chocolate Syrup with a splash of milk in the bottom of a glass and fill it the rest of the way with a diet cola. Sip through a straw.

If you're a bad "chocoholic" (like me) you may have a deficiency of iodine. Take one tablet, only one, of kelp with your morning vitamins.

Here is the recipe for my favorite breakfast: Pour six ounces of milk in a blender. (I like the two percent), add a banana, calorie-free chocolate syrup, five yellow packets of sweetener, and six ice cubes, then blend into a frothy, chocolate drink that has no more calories than the milk and the banana. (Bananas are so sweet and creamy that they taste fattening but aren't.)

Weight Watcher's "Giant Chocolate Cookies And Cream" ice cream bars are rich, delicious, and only one hundred and thirty calories.

Frozen grapes are sweet, crunchy, and as much fun to eat as candy. And good for you.

For another frozen fruit dessert, leave a grapefruit in the freezer for an hour.

If some particular high-calorie food is your nemesis, Vienna pastry for example, you might try aversion therapy. Lay in a four-days supply of whatever it is and eat that and nothing else. Just stuff it down till it's coming out of your nose. After a few days of forced feeding, you should be cured of the craving.

Never visit an all-you-can-eat buffet. Even *Gandhi* would stuff himself at one of those, trying to get his money's worth. If several of your friends are going to such a restaurant, you should be able to tag along for the company and make an agreement with the waiter that you will only consume, and pay for, one bowl of soup. A hearty chowder can satisfy like a full meal.

When you're hungry for something but don't know what you're hungry for, it's usually tomato juice.

Don't ever keep eating after you've had enough, just to "clean up your plate." That wholesome mid-western custom could add a hundred pounds over the years. What to do with a partially-finished meal? Slip a plastic bag over the plate and put it in the refrigerator to re-heat later. Give it to the dog. Give it to the birds. Give it to your garden.

Affirmations to repeat:

"I hate feeling stuffed."

"I won't eat until my stomach is actually growling from hunger then I'll stop when I'm not hungry anymore."

"I don't want to disturb my taste buds with anything that isn't top quality."

"I won't touch supermarket pastries."

"I can't eat junk food."

"No empty calories for me."

"Refined flour and sugar make me feel yucky."

If you use more than one supplement (I take eight.), use nail polish to mark the top of each bottle with the number of pills you take from it every morning.

Most of the humongously fat people we see aren't gluttons. They simply lack the gene you and I have that tells us we've had enough to eat. They can consume a whole plate of meat and potatoes and still feel hunger pangs, so have to stuff down more. Medical science has not yet discovered an artificial way to induce that natural condition of feeling full and satisfied.

Gastric bypass operations and stomach stapling are usually effective, but they are not the "easy" way to trim down. They are very expensive, difficult, painful, and dangerous and only to be resorted to if one's excess weight imminently threatens her life.

Let's assume the operation is a raging success with no complications. After the patient's stomach is stapled or rerouted, so she can only eat a thimbleful at a time, the pounds will come off. Then her extra belly skin will be hanging down to her knees and she will have to go back to the hospital to get that sliced off, get her navel cut out, repositioned and sewn back in. Maybe her breasts will be swinging down past her belt-line too, so those have to be carved up, the nipples cut out, repositioned and sewn back on. Then the excess skin on her arms and legs has to sliced off too.

Sweating Into Shape

If your doctor recommends a regimen of exercise, devise a program that will return a maximum of benefit for a minimum of unpleasant effort. Some exercise is fun, like dancing, riding horses, swimming, and golf. I like to take long walks through the city. My best friend, Louise, enjoys doing her errands on a bicycle My sister, Mary, is faithful to an early morning exercise show with someone named "Denise".

For a large-boned and well-muscled mesomorph, weight training should work best. For about fifty bucks you can buy a second-hand barbell set with instructions for your thrice weekly work-outs. Go at it.

If you have small bones, small muscles, and a tendency to put on fat, then you're an endomorph (like me) for whom a steady aerobic exercise will work wonders. I used to recommend jogging, but after years of huffing and puffing though the city streets, I wore down the cartilage in my knees. (If you spotted me trying to climb stairs without the aid of a hand rail and going, "Ow! Ow! Ow!" you would understand.) Now I suggest a low-impact or no-impact aerobic workout like walking, swimming, or cross-country skiing. Or *pretend* cross-country skiing on a Nordic Track.

A skinny ectomorph probably needs only twenty minutes a day of yoga or calisthenics for spot reducing. Do sit-ups to tame the tummy, leg lifts for the thighs, etc.

If your bottom is too flat, take up skating or do arabesques to round it out.

Make-Up

Our magazines abound in cosmetology lessons, illustrated with elaborate color charts, in the interest of helping you attract men. And not incidentally to sell cosmetics.

Well, never you mind, dear.

There isn't a worthwhile heterosexual man in the world who cares whether or not you shadow your cheekbones, highlight your brow, or apply just an eensy dab of blusher to your chin. The typical male is a crude barbarian and tends not to notice details. (Most of them can barely tell blue from green.) And it would never occur to him that your nose is slightly flat near the bridge or your bottom lip is fuller than the top. He simply takes in an over-all impression and judges favorably or unfavorably at first sight.

Cleanliness, energy, and self-confidence will make you more alluring to the opposing gender than the most painstaking art of expensive cosmeticians.

On the other hand, if it's women or gay men you want to look nice for, go ahead and sit on your bathroom sink and play with your paint box for an hour or so. They will appreciate it.

Most women need just a smidge of make-up to show regard for their place in the civilized world. For casual daytime, your morning toilette can take less than a minute. Use a big, fluffy brush to apply some blusher, then pink lipstick. If you work in an office or have a job dealing with the public, you may need a liquid base to even out skin tone.

But incandescent is the most flattering artificial light. So you can't make up by the bulb over your medicine chest and be sure you've got it covered.

For a day in the office under florescent lamps, you'll probably need more pink in your foundation. You could apply it under the florescent light in the ladies room at work. If you're going to be outdoors, shlep your magic colors over to the window and put them on under real sunlight. Make-up must be minimal, even undetectable, during the day or you will get known as "that lady who wears so much make-up". A foundation that accomplishes this artifice can cost twenty bucks a bottle. But after sundown, you can get away with almost anything.

Looking gorgeous for a marathon social event, like a wedding, requires specialized products. A stage performer's make-up has to stay vivid for hours under hot lights, so theatrical cosmetics cost less, have more pigment, and last longer than those formulated for the general public. I recommend Ben Nye brand cream foundation, blushers and eye-liner pencils.

After you apply the make-up, you must dust your art work with setting powder so it will stick all evening. But be aware that heavy make-up clogs the pores, so take it off with wet wipes the second you get home, and let your skin breathe again. Maybe as soon as you get back to your car.

Instant facial scrub: to a tablespoon of cheap cold cream, add a teaspoon of table salt. There's your scrub.

And take Christie Brinkley's advice: "The best beauty secret is *sunblock*."

Nails

It's worth noting that no normal man is compellingly drawn to inch-long finger nails, lacquered a bright crimson. Such obsessively-cultivated talons are more likely to call up an image of chicken claws dipped in blood than that of the sensuous Mandarin concubine you may be trying for. Keep your nails just long enough to scratch. Yourself or others. Any longer would be dysfunctional.

And there are too many vital tasks fake nails render impossible, like opening the clasp of a piece of jewelry.

I don't mean to put that charming Vietnamese lady at the nail salon out of business. I suggest only that you go more often, spend less time and money on each visit, and just get your natural nails a good polish that won't chip before the day is over.

Men like unpainted nails just fine so long as they're clean. Make certain of this by washing your dishes just before leaving on a date. This practice is quicker and more efficient than using a nail brush.

Fragrance

Something you will have to spend money on is perfume should you choose to wear it at all. The cheap stuff smells great for the first four minutes you have it on, then begins to reek like a toilet in a triple-X movie house. Audition any new fragrance by spraying yourself with the counter sampler. Then ride up and down in a crowded elevator and note the reactions.

Warning: More people than you would ever realize are allergic to scents.

State Of Mane

I have been unpleasantly surprised in some salons. The receptionist would quote a price, for say, a cut and style, and it sounded reasonable. But when I got the bill at the end of the visit, it was for nearly twice as much. When I asked for an accounting, they said, oh!, of course they had to charge me extra for the shampoo, the cream rinse, conditioning, combing, setting, and blowing dry. The remedy is to ask the fee for the work you want done and pay in advance. Show the receipt to your operator and advise her not to do anything that isn't already covered. That will prevent her from adding outrageously expensive services without warning then surprising you with the total.

Another economy measure is to shop where the professional beauticians do. I patronize a "Sally Beauty Supply" and pay five bucks a year to join the club so I can buy my hair products at a discount.

If your hair is too thin or fine, always get it cut under a full moon for maximum thickness. If your hair is too, too thick and you want it to grow longer and thinner, get it cut under a new moon.

Some women of African descent have committed mayhem on their hair from the time they were little girls. They started with braids that were too tight and weakened the root. Then there were corn rows that were also too tight. (Here's a tip: If it hurts, it's way too tight.) In their teen years, they graduated to hot combs and harsh straightening chemicals which also attacked the hair roots. By the time they hit middle age, their hair has become so thin that one could see their whole scalp through it, so they resort to wigs which don't allow the hair roots to breathe.

They blame genetics or "bad hair", but it's the abuse. Fortunately, most African women have very well-shaped heads and strong features, so they're striking in a classic short natural, which style doesn't strain the roots.

In a recent "Miss Universe" Pageant, "Miss Tanzania" didn't have any hair at all. Even bald, she was still beautiful enough to make it into the top ten finalists. She didn't *need* hair. (Whereas *I* need all the hair I can *get*.)

Do You Love Long Hair?

Nearly all icons of modern beauty: pageant contestants, centerfold girls, lingerie models, and TV and film temptresses are enhanced by long hair, collar-bone to bra length being the most common. Long hair is the most versatile to work with. It can be spectacular, waving and hanging loose, elegant, swept up in a chignon, or pulled back into a bun for a severe, professional look. But if you want your hair to grow as long as it can be, don't wear rollers to bed which puts the roots under tension. And you must let bangs and layers grow out so it becomes all one length.

Anyone can lengthen her hair with extensions, but they are very expensive, take a lot of time and upkeep, and damage the hair you have. So you shouldn't resort to extensions until you're sure you can't grow your own.

If you're descended from one of the fabulous-hair ethnic groups: Asians, Native Americans, Polynesians, etc. you can grow it as long and thick and lustrous as you like with no trouble. If you're undiluted Northern European (like me) you have to spend time and money to achieve the most beautiful "mane" in your circle.

When I decided to get serious about growing mine, I became a disciple of Dr. George Michael, who is the international guru of long hair care. (And no relation to the sexually-adventurous singer.) The most effective hair conditioning treatment is available at a George Michael salon, but I have none within a day's driving distance so often settle for a hot oil treatment at home. I drench my hair in olive oil then tuck it under a net and wear an electric heating cap, on the lowest setting, for an hour. (I bought the heating cap in a beauty supply shop for about twenty bucks. Less than one salon treatment.) I shampoo the oil out with one good lathering, then set and dry under a bonnet dryer on its lowest setting. My hair comes out looking thicker and healthier.

Dr. Michael advises that you never subject your hair to a temperature hotter than 108 degrees, that is ten degrees above body temperature. Letting your hair dry naturally is best but you can't do that when you have rollers in. A bonnet dryer on the lowest setting is second best. Blow dryers are too hot to use except for emergencies.

He also tells us to "shampoo hair as necessary" meaning only when it's actually dirty. Don't scrub away at your head every time you take a shower just to prove you're a clean person. You would be removing vital natural oils.

Certainly, the longer and older your hair is, the more dryness and split ends will occur but don't just give up and cut it short. Instead, after conditioning with George Michael products, shampooing, and towel drying, apply a small amount of Wildroot Hair Groom to the troublesome ends and allow to dry naturally. Also effective are jojoba oil and olive oil.

Bill Mahavier, the proprietor of George Michael Of Dallas, assessed my fine, tinted, hair and advised: "Whatever grooming product you buy, make sure it has no alcohol in it and no 'cones' like silicone, dimethicone, or trimethicone."

Wildroot Hair Groom meets those criteria. I get my neighborhood pharmacist to order it for me.

Mahavier also recommends a natural all boar-bristle hair brush which is kinder to your hair than any man-made product. And make sure the boar bristles aren't "reinforced" with nylon ones.

If your hair is long and thin and you want it to look thicker, you can cheat by braiding in yarn, ribbons, colored shoelaces, even a scarf.

Don't wear a wig or a hat for more than two hours at a time as your scalp has to breathe.

To avoid split ends, wear your long hair up and out of

harm's way except for "show off" occasions. A "scrunchie" is ideal for containing it, safer and gentler than any kind of elastic. (I know that Sarah Jessica Parker in "Sex In The City" said no real New York woman would ever wear a scrunchie, but New Yorkers don't know everything. These are people who pay seventy bucks for a t-shirt and a million for a two-bedroom apartment.)

Never brush wet hair. Wide-tooth comb only.

Never detangle with a brush or comb. Fingers only.

The supplements I take for healthy hair are flaxseed oil, biotin, iron, and brewer's yeast.

Would-be Rapunzels must eschew conventional hairdressers. Most are inclined to chop your hair off up to your ears then put a ton of spray or gel on what's left, blow it dry and scramble it like eggs so it looks like the top of a pineapple plant. You will walk out of the salon looking very chic but it would be impossible to achieve that style by yourself at your bathroom sink. Most salon "do's" don't survive one night's sleep.

I won't let anyone near my head with the sharp, pointy, things but a George Michael specialist, because I'm confident they won't take more than necessary. When they finish cutting, there isn't enough hair on the floor to fill a demitasse.

I enjoy the feel of my long hair on my back, a sensual pleasure without calories. On many a sweltering New Orleans evening, I walk around the house wearing nothing but undies and my hair.

Raiment

I have my own rule for clothes. They should be gorgeous if you're plain and simple if you're gorgeous. When the lady and the dress are both traffic-stopping, the overall effect is not stunning, but garish.

However, if you can't be pretty, you can always make a great appearance by being chic, as the plain and mannish Duchess of Windsor demonstrated so famously. This requires money or taste or both.

When you go to your closet and say, "Gee, I wish I had a: white blouse,.. blue shirt,... denim skirt,..." whatever, write the needed item down and go out and *get* one.

How to select an article of clothing: try it on and look in the dressing room mirror. If you never want to take it off again, buy it.

Never let the price vote on the purchase, or you will have a closet full of "bargain" items you don't care to wear. The price has veto power only.

In the interest of comfort, mobility, and your circulation, dress the size you are, and not the size you wish you were. If you're ashamed of that number 18 on the label, tear it out and sew in a 14. We won't tell.

(And select pantyhose at least one size larger than the sizing panel indicates. Life will be so much easier.)

You can buy beautiful, expensive, clothes at charity thrift shops, where the rich women turn in their duds to get a tax deduction. You must examine finds carefully for stains and moth holes, but don't be put off because a piece looks a little used. No one can tell whether a previous owner put some wear on it or you yourself did. If you bump into some society lady at a party who is rude enough to charge, "Why, that used to be *my* dress!" you should smile sweetly and say, "I love it. I'm so glad you outgrew it."

Then walk away before she has a chance to think of a rejoinder.

There is no "full disclosure" rule of dressing. You are free to keep all your worst parts covered and show only the good stuff. Long skirts were made for me as I have awful legs.(I'm the house model for Steinway.) And at my mature, slightly plump, time of life, I can push up and show off my bosoms. (Only where and when it's tasteful, of course, not for work-a-day.)

I believe in the "Color Me Beautiful" books. They demonstrate that your most flattering colors will make you appear younger and prettier. If you look best in black and snow white, you're a "winter". Wear the most vivid true colors. If you're gorgeous in pumpkin, you're an "autumn." Wear the fall colors: oranges, greens and browns. Warm, soft colors like coral and salmon are flattering on golden-skinned "springs." If you look best in pink and other pastels on the cool side, you're a "summer." (Like me, you lucky thing.)

Among men, the most usual favorite color is blue, if you care.

Tip: The right hat is the perfect finish to a "look". If you wear an eight-hundred-dollar suit, you may be noticed. But if you wear a fifty-dollar suit and a three-hundred-dollar hat, you will very *surely* be noticed.

Another tip from the wise old crone: I recommend sleeping in jogging clothes instead of pajamas. They're just as comfortable and when someone knocks on your door at the ungodly hour of ten or eleven a.m., they won't say, "Lord, that slattern was still asleep!" but, "What a fitness buff. She must have just come in from jogging."

Buy men's jogging pants which are sturdier than ours and have better pockets.

Furs

The only furs a woman really needs are a mink jacket and a full-length mink coat in classic colors and styles. Those two pieces will get you through any winter. (Don't bother with a stole; they're too much trouble to hold on to.) The highest-quality minks are the let-out female pelts from North America. Scandinavian minks are heavier because they have thicker leather. If you spend a lot of time indoors in your coat, say shopping in a mall, you could overheat and faint in a too-heavy garment

Mink is the only luxury fur that is also durable and a marvelous investment, because if you take care of it, send it to cold storage every spring, it will last your whole life.

Whenever you wear any fur, you must have a new garbage

bag, neatly folded, in the pocket. In case of rain, the fur goes into the bag.

The best closet "storage bag" for a fur is an old cotton sheet fastened around it with safety pins.

"Something big in a little blue box from Tiffany's."
Elizabeth Taylor on being asked what it would take to win her attention.

Jewelry

A beautiful young woman doesn't need jewelry. Sparklers may only distract from her own living charms.

But anyone past thirty might invest in one grand-looking piece to wear every day. Perhaps a fine watch or ring that looks like an heirloom. You don't have to spend a fortune. Pawn shops make you good deals on jewelry. Patronize one that will give you full credit for a trade-in, then every time you get a few hundred bucks ahead, you can run in and upgrade your finger.

Semi-precious stones give you a lot of sparkle for less. Garnets are as red as rubies. White sapphires look like diamonds. Shop-at-home channels have beautiful peridots and citrines and other semi-precious stones you can afford in an impressive carat weight. (I love the Victoria Wieck designs.)

You can buy jewelry on a "flex-plan" which will space out the payments over three or four credit card bills. Maybe your husband won't notice. (Hoping he doesn't examine the monthly statements as closely as mine does.)

Gems are no fun if they don't sparkle. The low-cost method is to put your rings in a rocks glass, cover them with ammonia and agitate them by hand for five minutes. Then scrub with an old toothbrush. If you rinse your jewelry at the sink, always put a wash cloth over the drain first.

And by all means, get as many baubles as you can as presents. They hold their value and are more easily liquidated during lean times than flowers or candy. But the expensive pieces must live in your safe deposit box. Take out one at a time only to wear on a heavy date with the gentleman who bought them for you.

And don't array yourself with Newton's gifts when you're out with Sid. If Sid wants to escort rubies and emeralds, he should spring for them himself.

Your Public Image

Don't let the most noticeable thing about you be something that isn't a compliment.

"She's the girl who always wears purple," is not a compliment

"She's always doing something interesting," *is* a compliment.

You should always give the impression that your life is rich and adventurous. If it isn't, you can make it appear so. Take advantage of whatever recreational or cultural facilities your area offers, just so it seems that you're doing something. Even an evening at the community theater or a motor trip to your state forest qualifies as something.

Take a cordon bleu cooking course. Fix up your house and put it on the neighborhood tour. Buy a boat; men *love* boats. Spend a year in Europe or with the Peace Corps. Write a book. (Not this one.)

Join a political campaign. If you say you worked for a presidential candidate, winning or losing, you make a favorable impression and it's also a good way to get party invitations. You don't have to mention that all you did was stuff envelopes in a neighbor's kitchen.

If you have a houseguest you can brag about, go ahead and brag. "It's my friend Jonne. Just finished a show on Broadway and she's taking a month off." Or "They're mortgage bankers from up north. They simply insisted on taking me to Commander's Palace."

If your visitor is just dotty Aunt Mildred or your ten-year - old niece, you keep her identity a tantalizing secret. "Oh, no one you would know."

Let your date imagine Princess Caroline of Monaco popped in for the night.

Be mysterious, too, about your mundane pastimes. Do not admit you're just staying home to watch "Law & Order" reruns. And be sure to screen your calls. If you answer the phone at eight pm, your suitor will know you're not museum-hopping but just hunkered down, doing your nails and watching "Lenny Briscoe" make wisecracks to a "mope".

Make the most of networking encounters. You can get into a posh fund-raiser where famous people will be present. If you can't afford a ticket, go in as an assistant florist or carrying sound equipment. Have your friend, Louise, follow you around with a camera. Run up to each famous person in turn and gush your gratitude for the wonderful work he or she is doing while Louise jumps in and snaps your picture. You display the photos around your office and visitors will assume you know the famous people. They won't pin you down for details, though, because they won't want to admit they're impressed.

At one of a myriad of mystery conferences I've attended, there was a plump, vivacious redhead I'll call "Beatrice" who was on tour with her new novel. She was brimming with verve and confidence and looked like a star. I was very impressed. We all were.

"Who published your book?" I asked.

"Smythe-Grimsby Press" she replied, earnestly.

I hadn't heard of the publisher but figured it was one of those chic new imprints so was snookered into buying the book. Then when I got it home and tried to read it, saw that the novel was pure drivel.

Who would publish this tripe? I wondered.

A Google search revealed that "Smythe-Grimsby Press" was mentioned only three times on the whole world wide web and all in reference to Beatrice's book. She had *self*-published the dreck! And she was not distinguished enough in and of herself to have ever been mentioned anywhere outside her high school yearbook. By the time anyone realized that the lady's resume was empty, she had garnered all the invitations, speaking engagements, and other perks of being a prominent author.

She had simply made up a name that sounded like an old-line publishing company out of Boston or Philadelphia, printed up her own claptrap in hardcover, and presented herself as a novelist. The moral of that story is that chutzpah can trump real accomplishment. Maybe you and I ought to get some of that there.

NOTE: Be sure to keep most of your image *from* the public. That is, don't ever pose naked for anyone, anywhere. Or those pictures will end up on the internet forever and your great-grandchildren will be snickering at them.

CHAPTER TWENTY-THREE: COPING WITH MENSTRUATION

Sometimes a napkin just isn't enough.

During those icky days when you find yourself going through wads of toilet paper and rinsing out your scanties every five minutes, you may look for drastic solutions.

One new product you may want to consider is the old-fashioned sponge. Perfectly natural and organic, the sponge can be washed out after each use and kept as part of your feminine hygiene program throughout many monthly cycles.

Okay, sisters, enough of that.

The chapter heading and paragraphs above were only a diversion calculated to gross out any males nosy enough to read this book. The reason for getting rid of them will become obvious. This section deals with self-defense.

The subject of assault is a uniquely repellent one and I didn't want to write this chapter but the book would have been incomplete without it.

The reality is that every woman everywhere, regardless of age or description, must assume she will be targeted for attack one day. (As I write this, my local news is showing the mug shot of a large, beefy man who was just arrested for raping an eighty-two-year-old Alzheimer's patient.) So plan well in advance how to respond.

Your womanly scream is your best weapon. A self-defense instructor will tell you that in fifty percent of the cases, a loud noise alone is enough to fend off an attack. I studied voice so have a nice loud scream which has saved me on at least five occasions that I remember, here in mid-city New Orleans.

One night, very late, I was roused from a light sleep by the sound of a man creeping through my bungalow. I screamed so loud that I was hoarse for days. (That was before I studied voice.) The burglar grabbed my purse off my dresser and fled back through the window he had entered by. No one heard me but the burglar himself but he didn't know that and ran off without attacking me.

Some self-described "authorities" recommend that you not resist a mugger. "If a stranger accosts you on the street, ask him what he wants," they advise ingenuously. "If it's your wallet he's after, hand it over. It's not worth fighting over money."

Nu?! Sure, you can afford to lose your wallet. But the mugger isn't on the honor system. He may take the money then kill you out of rage because there wasn't enough to make the robbery worth his while. Or because you couldn't get your rings off fast enough. Or to prevent you from identifying him, even if you *wouldn't* be able to identify him.

This wise old crone's recommendation is simple and obvious. Don't *let* the stranger accost you on the street.

Your first defense is eternal caution. Look around you constantly to check the terrain. In a light traffic area, you may walk down the middle of the street so no one can jump out at you from the cover of an alley or doorway. Don't count on hearing footsteps. Street criminals usually wear sneakers and have learned to run silently. Imagine that you are confronted by a man with a large knife. Or a large man with a small knife. There is one element that can protect you even from a gorilla with a machete and that is *distance*. Nobody can assault you from half a block away, and you must not allow a strange man to get any closer than that in an unsecured area. If you see someone approaching on your side of the street, cross to the other. If he then steps off the curb to follow you, do not wait there for him on the chance that he's just a nice guy needing directions to Our Lady Of Perpetual Help but speed up and stay well out of his reach. Fill your lungs and let out the loudest, shrillest scream you know how to do while he is still way over *there*, because once he's within grabbing distance, you won't be able to scream. He probably won't want to give away his intentions by running after you. If he does, though, raise the sleeping and the dead by screaming at full volume. A criminal's instinct is to run away from, not toward, a noise like that.

A battery-operated bullhorn may be even better for high-decibel communication because you can broadcast your peril in great detail. "Help, help! I'm being chased by two men on eight hundred block, Howard Street." In the unlikely event that your molesters don't turn tail and run at that, you can elaborate. "One is tall and blond with a blue jacket and the other is short with black hair and a scar across his nose."

If the noise doesn't stop an attacker and you can't outrun him, you might roll under a parked truck or SUV, still screaming. You can also throw a rock through a store window to set off the burglar alarm. Then when the police come, tell them the mugger did it and describe him.

If, on this hypothetical lonely street, you see two men casually approaching you from two different directions, then run like a rabbit in a *third* direction. Because those two men are confederates, split up to seem less threatening. Bet on it.

And don't expect to be alerted to danger by the sight of a growling, flailing, brute. A criminal is just as likely to be well spoken, clean-cut, and nicely dressed, collegiate, even. (Ted Bundy looked like a guy you would date, and would put his arm or leg in a phony cast to appear absolutely harmless.)

A thug may stroll along with his hands in his pockets, whistling a merry tune, or pretending to look for a house number as an excuse to approach you and ask the way. Predators often scope a victim out while chatting amiably.

"Hi, I'm waiting for my sister, Cleo. She has a dance class in this building."

Do not feel constrained to act friendly toward every man you see.

"But if I deliberately avoid him, he'll be offended. He'll think I'm a snob."

Never mind; you don't owe it to anyone to show trust by placing your life in his hands.

Unless you are running for office or it's part of your job, you have no compelling reason to talk to any man who hasn't been properly introduced.

Cautionary Tales

A hotel guest had just reached her suite when the phone rang. "Hello, Ma'am? This is the front desk. We heard there's water leaking from your bathroom sink into the room below you. I'm sending a man up there to fix it." The caller wasn't the front desk clerk but a rapist on a house phone, sending *himself* up to the woman's room, dressed as a workman.

A local woman had just finished shopping in a mall and was safely back in her car when a stranger appeared at the driver's side window, holding up a five-dollar bill. "You dropped this," he said. The shopper knew she hadn't dropped any money so just shook her head and started the engine. Then the stranger began screaming at her and pounding on the window.

If a man manages to get in your car and demands that you drive off, gun or no, do not drive off. Crash the car instead. Your seat belt and air bag will save you.

Three blocks from my house, a woman was waiting for a bus at high noon, when a teenager approached her and pulled his t-shirt up over his face. She thought maybe he was taking the t-shirt off because he was hot, but he was just using it to cover his face while he robbed her. The t-shirt over the face has become the warm-weather equivalent of the ski mask. When you see that gesture, scream for all you're worth and run.

Many criminals work bus stops. One trick is to wait till you've ascended the bus then jump on after you, snatch your purse, and run. This happened to me once, but luckily, I was holding my purse too tight. The criminal in that case, one of a swarm, was about nine years old.

When you see a man at your bus stop, wait up the block or across the street. And let all male riders ascend the bus before

202

you do.

Don't carry a purse anyway. A woman's reflex is to hold onto the flipping thing even while fighting for her life, reducing her natural resisting power by ninety percent. A purse is no good as a weapon unless it's filled with weights and you're an expert at swinging it. Put your keys, change and lipstick in your pocket. Wrap an elastic around your credit card, driver's license, a couple of checks and a twenty dollar bill and stick them in your other pocket and secure it with a big safety pin. You can hook your phone on your belt.

Don't get in an elevator if you're leery of its contents. If a man steps in after you, step right out again and wait for the next elevator.

Tact could kill you.

If you can't, gracefully or ungracefully, divest yourself of a stranger's company, you might squint and pretend you know him from somewhere.

"Excuse me. I think I've met you before. What's your name?"

If he says "Earl," come right back with, "Earl what? I may know your family." Or "Weren't you at the supermarket with a heavyset lady?"

(Everyone in the country was at some time in some supermarket with some heavyset lady.)

Most women don't risk walking down the street alone at night, so the criminals have the extra bother of coming into their homes after them. And often the victims invite them in. One assailant's tactic is to knock on your door and introduce himself as a policeman. He reports that your husband or child has been in an accident. You, in a fit of anguish, leave your door open while you run for your purse. Then the "policeman" steps in after you and does whatever he likes.

Don't open your door to anyone unless you're expecting him. If someone rings your bell claiming an official capacity, call the agency that sent him for verification. Look up the number in your phone book; don't take it from him.

A man in the house is a good security feature. A big dog in the house is better. Even a small dog can alert you to danger, so get yourself a stalwart combination burglar alarm and body-guard of any breed. Or no breed. Yes, she involves trouble and expense, but if Poochie prevents even one burglary, she will have earned her kibble and flea treatments for five years. If she saves you from being assaulted or murdered, she will earn it for life.

A lock on your bedroom door will greatly reduce your chance of waking up with a knife at your throat. If you make frequent trips to the bathroom, keep an old-fashioned chamber pot under your bed and keep that door locked. Of course, you have your cell phone on your bed table. A criminal can cut the wires on a land line or just lift the receiver off an extension, dis-abling all the phones on the circuit.

If you hear running water outside your house, a criminal may have turned on your outside faucet so you will step out and investigate.

When you buy an expensive new appliance, do *not* adver-tise your acquisition by leaving the empty box outside for the trash pick-up.

Always keep your phone and house keys with you, in your pocket while you're awake, by your bed while you sleep.

Be Your Own Hero

You're more likely to be attacked by someone you know than by a stranger, though less likely to report it. To avoid an unpleasant surprise on a date, don't allow your escort to drive you to a place so distant or isolated that you can't get back by yourself. The "Put out or get out" routine is a cliché but not a joke.

Suppose an acquaintance tricks you into his car for "a spin to the pizza place" then suddenly turns off down a long, unfami-liar road and speeds up. If you are securely seat-belted, you can swing open your door. He can not reach over far enough to close it while driving and he won't continue driving with the door hanging open like that. So he'll have to stop the car and you can run. But this won't work if the driver can lock all the doors from his seat or if he has removed the passenger's door handle. Should you be imprisoned inside the car, you can pull something out of the glove compartment and heave it out the window, defecate and/or vomit all over the upholstery or burn it with the dashboard lighter.

If hand-to-hand combat is necessary, make your end of it feet. Keeping your seat belt fastened, swing your legs over and kick at him furiously, screaming like a maniac all the while. Your legs are longer and stronger than your arms and probably stronger than *his* arms.

A predator may shoot your tire out with a twenty-two, then just as you're wringing your hands over the "blow-out", appear like a good Samaritan and offer to help. Then, while you're bubbling with gratitude, he will shove you inside the car and assault you.

Another predator's trick is to deliberately bump your car so you get out to ask for his insurance information. In that case, either call 911 from inside your car or drive to the nearest police station or well-secured area to report the accident.

Thank providence for the invention of the cell phone. You can keep your windows rolled up and call your auto club. If you don't have a cell phone, put on your hazard lights to alert the highway patrol to stop and call for help for you.

If you are attacked by someone you know, it is even more important to fight back. Don't pound your little fists against his big chest and biceps unless you're just trying to be cute because he'll barely feel it. But concentrate on marking him with your trusty nails. If there is no visible evidence that you resisted his attack, his defense attorney will claim you invited it.

When a house cat is cornered by a dog many times her size, and with much longer teeth, she doesn't ever go limp and weep for mercy. Rather, she unsheathes her trusty claws and slashes for all she's worth while giving out with a howl so blood-curdling as to unnerve the most murderous hound.

Women and cats, unlike men and dogs, have been endowed with superior flexibility (to writhe free from a predator's grasp), sharp claws, and piercingly shrill voices to compensate for their lack of muscle and bulk. But the woman, unlike the cat, may be too psyched out to employ her survival mechanisms. Take a page from Tabby's book and flee at the slightest sign of danger. But if you can't get away, go for the eyes and scream until you're blue in the face. If you don't yell, you won't be heard. If you don't fight, you can't win.

If you get a good grip on the attacker's testicles, don't just give them a playful tug to show what you *could* do if you weren't such a nice girl. You don't make any points with an assailant by refraining from hurting him. You're playing for keeps, so crush those revolting spheroids *together. Hard.*

Should a man try to choke you, it's futile to try to loosen his hands with yours. You can break his grip by clasping your hands together in a double fist and suddenly throwing them up between his arms and over your head. He won't be able to hold on because your biceps are stronger than his thumbs. Then you might attack his eyes with your nails.

Rape crisis centers recommend "immediate aggressive resistance" on the part of any woman who is threatened.

Should you not fight back to the best of your ability, the first consequence is that you will, indeed, be raped. The second is even worse. Once the numbing fright wears off, you will feel a desperate anger at the violation. And since the guilty party won't be around to answer for it, you will turn your anger inward, hating yourself for your "cowardice" even more than you will hate the rapist. Though you were, quite naturally, paralyzed with fear at the time and unable to react. Women who are more frightened than angry will go limp. Women who get angry at their attackers fight back. But, as mentioned before, the anger often doesn't erupt till *after* the attack. Anger gives you speed and strength and you should be able to call up that virulent emotion at the times when you most need it.

A good way to get your blood racing is to shout, a grand and bellicose roar of rage. If you're too scared or too distracted to feel angry at the mugger yet, try to think of someone who *does* stimulate your violent instincts and transfer them.

"Why, Nate, you mother-#@&*%! You took every last stick of furniture in the house! After I put you through CCNY! Cleared out my bank account!..." etc. It may disconcert the mugger to be railed at this way. He knows he's not Nate and isn't in any mood to deal with a foul-mouthed crazy woman. (How unfeminine!) But his confusion won't hurt your case. Just keep railing and flailing. The last thing he wants is a fight.

Above all understand that you are alone in such a crisis and you have only seconds to decide how to come through it with as little damage as possible. In any attack you survive, you can say you dealt with it successfully.

The "Gentleman Rapist"

The police classify a "gentleman rapist" as a man, usually an acquaintance, who forces himself on you, threatening you with a weapon, maybe his fist, ordering you to take your own clothes off so there won't be any sign of a struggle, then, *afterward,* acts exactly as if the sex were consensual and a delightful romantic encounter for both of you. He'll speak soothingly to calm you down and help you get dressed and pulled back together. He can't have you falling out of his car half-naked and hysterical. He may apologize for "rushing things" and even cry pitifully that he couldn't help "making love" to you because you're so beautiful and that you were responsible for "sending mixed signals". He will express concern for your safety, escort you home, and even ask for another "date".

There is nothing a man can say or do *after* an assault that would make it *not* an assault. Just pretend you believe him, then go into your house and call the police and the rape crisis center.

Once you go public with his attack, other women are likely to come forward to say he did the exact same thing to *them*.

Alarm Systems

Popular commercial: A harried housewife hears the glass breaking out of her back door and the alarm shrieks "Wee-ooo, Wee-ooo, Wee-ooo!" and lights blink. Then the phone rings. Shivering with fear, wifey picks up the receiver and a calm male voice at the other end says, "Are you all right, Ma'am?"

"No," she whimpers. "Someone is trying to break in."

"I'll send the police," the hero assures.

"Oh, thank you!" the woman weeps with gratitude.

'S'cuse me? Since the helpless householder had her phone right at hand, she could have dialed 911 herself and summoned the police a lot faster if she hadn't wasted time explaining her situation to that monitor who was hunched over a computer screen somewhere in Northern Ohio. I saw a "real-crime" re-enactment on TV in which home invaders were holding a family hostage. One aunt had escaped unnoticed and crept down the hall, pushed the emergency alarm button, then scampered back into hiding. The monitors didn't call the police. Instead, according to their policy, they called the house back to say someone had entered an alarm at that address. If the invaders had answered the phone, they would have known there was one family member they hadn't caught and gone after her. Fortunately, the aunt managed to hurry down the hall and answer the phone herself. She would have been better off using the phone in the first place and punching 911 instead of the alarm button which almost got her killed.

Home security companies aren't really interested in selling the bells and wires of the electronic systems. They get their real money from talking you into signing a two-year contract to have the system monitored, which they turn right around and sell to a monitoring service. You may assume you're dealing with a local firm but the monitors are probably in another region of the country.

All you really need is a good, loud, alarm system that would alert you to a break-in or a fire. It should be loud enough to be heard by a neighbor who would call the police for you if you're not at home. You and your neighbor should agree to be each other's monitors and save the monthly fee.

A burglar may come to the house and present himself as an employee of your security firm. He will offer you a "free upgrade" of your alarm system then come inside and disable it.

Video Protection

Detective Mike Carambat of the New Orleans Police Department advises us to place a small video camera outside the home, positioned low to record a clear picture of anyone who approaches. The little camera can be purchased on the internet for about ten bucks. You use your own computer to record hours of video and the software is free.

Bang-Bang

A few years ago, I didn't believe in firearms at all, wouldn't even have one in the house. But when my neighbor got beaten up in her front yard for her engagement ring, I rethought my policy.

Here in Louisiana, any law-abiding adult in good mental health is allowed to apply for a concealed-carry permit. So I took the mandatory firearms safety course, which included range time, submitted my fingerprints for a background check, and got my permit. Now I have a .38 special revolver for protection.

Some weekends on our farm, my husband nails an empty feed sack to a tree stump and I don my eye and ear protection and have some target practice. I have never fired at anything but a paper target and never want to. But those nights when I drag home alone after a late rehearsal, I'm a little less likely to be assaulted in my driveway.

(I think I heard someone say "Gee, Tony, if mid-city New

Orleans is so dangerous, why don't you and your husband just move out to that farm you have?"

Shut up. You sound like my husband.)

If a law-abiding citizen isn't allowed to carry a firearm in your area, find out what you *may* carry. Tear gas, pepper spray, or even a screech alarm is better than nothing.

In summation, your best protection from attack is distance. If you choose to carry a weapon, be sure to have it on you at all times and are able to act instinctively. No defense, either natural like your own God-given scream and fingernails, or otherwise, like mace or a firearm, will be of any help unless you're determined to use it.

One more caution: Whenever passing close to a man, even in broad daylight, always watch his hands. This is so he can't reach out and snatch a quick feel then run off hooting while you rage and fume helplessly.

"Manners is to do and say the kindest thing, the kindest way." Anonymous

CHAPTER TWENTY FOUR: FENNELLY'S CHARM SCHOOL

Charm is a behavior that can be learned like any other. If you don't have it, you can get it. It can be as simple as emphasizing the positive element of a situation.

If there is a college of charm, its Latin motto should be "Negan Nolite!", "Don't be negative!" Try to maintain a positive attitude about everything. If you can't, you can *act* as though you do.

If you can be happy for other people's good fortune, you will be happy much more often than if you can only be happy for yourself.

Even the poorest individual can be generous, at least with compliments. If someone deserves a compliment, confer one. For example, if someone has gotten all dressed up, she deserves a compliment.

The first rule is that your remark must be true. If you tell some dorky-looking guy he's handsome, that would be fawning. Mind you, he may believe it anyhow, but the people around you would lose all respect.

There is always something nice to say about a person. You may compliment a woman on her startlingly beautiful eyes. If she, somewhat sheepishly, admits that she's wearing tinted contacts, you can still compliment her on her color sense just as if she had chosen a flattering ensemble.

Little girls should always be complimented. If the child isn't pretty, you can call her something that *sounds* like pretty:

chic, elegant, vivacious, graceful...

But you can always call people "charming" because they are all willing to believe they are.

Be careful when describing someone. "Tall" is a compliment. "Short" isn't. Slim is a compliment; fat isn't. Young is a compliment; old isn't. Blond hair, gray hair, red hair, black hair are all acceptable descriptions. "Bald" is not acceptable unless the guy shaves his head in which case he's proud of being bald so it's okay to mention it. If you have to describe someone who is short, fat, and bald, describe his clothes instead.

"The man in the blue shirt and brown pants is waiting on me."

Do not describe yourself as "short" to someone who is even shorter, or as "fat" to someone who is even fatter, and so on.

You must not ask a woman if she's married, but you may ask her if she's single.

Don't feel obligated to reciprocate to a Christmas card that's merely a mass-mailed ad:

"Hi, Gang - Hope this card finds you and yours well and happy. We're busy preparing for the spring concert tour. You can find my latest CDs on my website..."

Thoughtfulness counts. You can give presents your friends would appreciate but won't actually cost you anything but a fond thought: a magazine with an article on their favorite subject, flowers or ferns from your garden, fresh eggs from your chickens. You know that silk blouse you bought on sale because you were positive you were going to lose weight but didn't, so never wore? It will fit your girlfriend, Claudine. (She's still a size eight, the bitch.)

When someone tells you his job, think of something positive to say about it:

"Great. Accounting pays very well, I hear."

"Waiting tables sure will keep you in shape."

"I'd like to be a night-watchman. Plenty of time to read."

"Picking up cans on the street is good for the environment."

Maybe all you can say is, "Sure beats going hungry."

When introduced to a new baby, you must gush, "Why he looks exactly like your husband!" even if the kid is a ringer for Colin Farrell.

How To Say Mean Things in the Nicest Way:

If a man's hair is receding, he has "an intelligent high forehead."

If it's mostly gone, it's "receding." If he's bald as a doorknob, you can say he looks like Patrick Stewart, or is a Kojak type, if he's swarthy, a Yul Brynner type if he's small, a Michael Jordan type if he's black. You don't have to think of one for American Indians: Those guys get to keep their hair. A small consolation from God for losing all their land.

A fat woman is "full-figured" or "ample."

A fat man is "sturdily-built" or "portly."

A short man is "compactly-built."

A shrimpy woman is "petite."

Your poor friends are "on a budget."

A drunk "enjoys a drink once in a while."

A slob is "casual about his appearance."

A tactless person is "refreshing."

A loudmouth is "out-spoken."

If a woman is dumb as mold, you can say she's "naive and trusting."

A dog with no manners is "playful."

Ditto a child with no manners.

Here is an example of a tactful response:

"What do you think of my uncle Howie?" (Uncle Howie is a fat, noisy, drunk.)

"Why I love his car." or "He sure has great taste in shoes."

What You Can Say When You Just Saw Your Friend, Edna, In A Terrible Play:

"Congratulations!"

"I would *never* have been able to remember all those

213

lines!"

"You look *gorgeous* in that dress!"

"I'll bet the critics will *rave* about it!" (Because most critics are pretentious twits who will praise anything they don't understand.)

"I'm so glad I came!" (Because I unselfishly showed my support for my good friend, Edna.)

"You shoulda been out *front!*"

Sometimes in social situations a little white lie is in order. Like "It was wonderful to see you again."

(If any of my friends is reading this, hey, I wasn't lying when I said it was wonderful to see *you* again. Not *you.*)

When ending a conversation, it's nice if you can thank the person for something:

"Thanks so much for the update/ good wishes/ good advice..."

When a friend asks you for a favor, say either "Yes":

"Sure. I'll do that right now." or "I'll make a note of that right now." And get out a piece of paper and write it down. Switch your watch to the wrong wrist to remind you.

Or "No.": "I wish I could, but I simply don't have the time/money/car."

Or "Maybe.": "I'm not sure I can. Call me tonight/tomorrow at ? o'clock and I'll tell you if I was able to get it done."

Believe me, your friend would rather be told "No," even rudely, than depend on you for something only to be disappointed.

When someone thanks you, try saying "You're welcome," instead of "No problem."

Members of minority groups don't like to be reminded of it, even if you're bestowing a compliment like, "You Jews are so smart." or "I wish I could dance like you black people."

An exception is us Irish Catholics. We're so proud of being Irish that we're happy to hear jokes about drinking and fighting and potatoes. Mind you, we lost our official minority status when one of our guys got elected president back in 1960. (Though none since, I've noticed.)

Are you awakened early on Saturday morning by earnest church ladies waving bible tracts? They mean well, so you don't want to be nasty to them. Instead, warn them away by posting a sign, "NO RELIGIOUS AGENTS" right over your door bell. If they ignore the sign, feel free to act annoyed.

Suppose you bring your delicious home-made fruit compote to a party and at the end of the evening, there is still some left in the bowl? If the event was held in a common venue, say a picnic ground or the church basement, of course you will take it home with you. But what if you're at Bethany's house? If Bethany would like that fruit compote for herself, it would be churlish to take it back. But what if she *doesn't* want it? She may just throw it out, the moment you leave.

So say, "I'll leave this fruit compote with you and you can have it for dessert tomorrow."

She will say either, "Oh, thank you! I *love* that fruit compote," or "No, take it home with you. I'm cutting out sweets this week."

If you brought a bottle of wine or spirits to Bethany's, you must leave it behind unless Bethany is a recovering alcoholic. *Except* if you were asked to "BYOB". Then, that's *your* "B."

Say you're at a book signing and one "fan" is taking up all your time, maybe not even buying a book but just asking advice on how to get her own drivel published while other people wait and wait on line.

Say, "Oh, shame on me! I've been enjoying talking to you so much that I'm neglecting everyone else. Would you like to take a copy to the cashier and come back and get it signed?"

Phone Manners

Voice-On-Phone: "Hello, is Tom there?"
You: "Who's calling?"
WRONG. That's rude. Let's try it again.

215

Voice-On-Phone: "Hello, is Tom there?"

You: "Yes. Shall I tell him who's calling?"

Voice-On-Phone: "Mary Foof."

You: "Just a minute – Tom? Mary Foof is on the phone."

Tom: "*&%#! I don't know anyone named Mary *&%#! Foof!"

You: (Back on phone.) "Tom can't come to the phone right now. Would you like to leave a message and he can get back to you?"

You see, admitting that Tom is on the premises doesn't obligate him to talk to the caller if he doesn't want to. Now it's Mary Foof's turn. She can leave a message he chooses to respond to:

"I'm the social secretary for his boss's wife. She would like to invite you both to a garden party next weekend."

Or one he doesn't: "I have a special offer, good this week only, for..."

When you are the caller, you can save time and suspicion by identifying yourself and your business immediately.

You As The Caller: "Hello, this is Margie Boo. Is Tom there? I'd like to ask him about the neighborhood association meeting tonight."

We can end a phone call gracefully with, "I've got to run and start dinner... feed the dog... get my groceries..." Don't admit you're just running to watch Ellen Degeneres do charades. That would be considered a frivolous reason to terminate this vital conversation.

TIP: Always check your cell phone to make sure your call is disconnected before mentioning what you really think of the person you just talked to.

How to break yourself from using dirty words.

Something I never heard any man say is: "I wish my girl had a foul mouth."

Whenever you catch yourself just starting to use the bad word, utter an invocation like "St. Anthony pray for us" three times. If you utter the whole word, say it six times. Mind you,

216

St. Anthony is *my* patron saint and you may use your own, of course. Or say "Next year in Jerusalem" or recite the AA serenity prayer. If you don't believe in any religion at all, just use your favorite affirmation.

Dining Out

Say your Tante Chlotilde invites you to join her and Nonc Verbus for Thanksgiving dinner. You feel obligated to go because Nonc Verbus helped put the tin roof on your shed last Summer. If you ask, "When should we come?" she'll reply "Two o'clock," knowing full well she won't be serving the turkey till eight and you will be stuck there for six hours, chopping offal for the dirty rice and keeping Nonc company while he watches television and he only watches football and fishing shows.

If you ask "What time will you be serving dinner?" Tante will *know* you want to accomplish as close to an "eat and run" as you can get away with and be insulted.

So ask only, "What time?"

Then she should feel obligated to mention the actual serving time.

"We'll be eating at eight, but you can come in the afternoon."

You reply, "Oh, that's wonderful! We'll get there as soon as we can."

You won't be able to manage that till seven-twenty-five. Bring a nice bottle of wine.

(Not a *box* of wine.)

Dull Parties

You *hate* Edna's parties. There's never anyone there but her relatives and not one of those losers can do you any good. But you have to put in an appearance.

Someone asked Orson Welles how he managed to leave an event without drawing attention to himself, big as he was and important as he was, and as famous as he was.

"Just empty yourself of all ego," Welles advised.

So your mission is to enter Edna's party flamboyantly and exit invisibly. Arrive early and park your car down the block so no one hears you start the engine to leave, or worse that you have to make a loud announcement that someone's car is blocking yours. Walk in, smiling and bubbling, praise everything in sight, then wait till the party is in full swing before you slip out the door. Later that evening, e-mail Edna about how wonderful the party was so she'll remember that you paid your respects.

"Thank you so much for inviting me. I loved your avocado dip."

If Edna brings up the fact that you left early, you can say, "I had to go home and put ice on my knee, but I'm so glad I had a chance to talk to your Aunt Minnie again... admire your Hummel collection... pet your Shar Pei."

Or you can pretend your phone is on vibrate, open it as you pull it out of your pocket, so no one sees that it wasn't lit up and pretend you're being summoned to an emergency.

"It's my husband/sister/room-mate. The dog got out and I have to help look for her."

Houseguesting

Some homeowners enjoy having company, but most people, especially your friends' husbands, would rather be left the hell alone to enjoy their "castles" in peace. So the net benefit of having you around has to outweigh the nuisance quotient. If you are too poor to contribute financially, you can pick up a dish rag.

"Oh, I just love to scour pots. Do you mind?"

If you're a celebrity, the cachet of having you there may be payment enough. If you're a cordon bleu cook, you can earn your board by whipping up a gourmet feast.

I am not a celebrity and don't have any money and abhor housework, so I usually "pay my way", in a manner of speaking, by giving my hostess an astrology reading. I don't have to carry my computer for this. There are some web sites that enable one to input birth data and calculate a chart, so all I have to do is print it out and provide the interpretation.

New York Magazine had an article about weekending in the Hamptons. (Most of their articles seem to be about that.) And one fashionable bachelor revealed that he was always welcome as a houseguest because he A: brought a hostess gift, B: took his hosts out to a good restaurant for dinner, and C: tipped the maid.

If you ever want to be invited back again, to the home of your hosts or to any of their friends', say only positive things about the accommodations. Even if the hosts smoked like chimneys, the mattress was lumpy and in the middle of the living room, and they didn't have cable. Maybe all that you can come up with is, "Your dog was adorable!" So say that.

If you're paying for the room, you have a right to complain. Or if the hospitality is in compensation for something, say partial payment for a speaking engagement, you're perfectly justified in saying, "I don't want to stay with Bert and Frieda again. They're both drunk by five P.M. and their ghastly kids kept me awake all night and their putrid dog kept jumping on me and muddying my clothes. And Bert made a pass at me in the kitchen. And Frieda made a pass at me in the dining room."

Your hosts should experience a net gain from your visit. If on your way out, you don't hear them trilling, "Please come back any time," maybe you didn't do it right.

For Shy People

When you go to a conference or a party, "the roof serves as your introduction." You have a common interest or common acquaintances with everyone present and are free to address anyone on that basis.

"Norma puts out a scrumptious feast."

"I'm so happy to see some of my favorite authors here."

"Isn't Bitsy lovely in her ball gown?"

"What a beautiful setting! Walter and Ben have so much taste."

The first rule is that your *opening* conversational gambit must be positive. The only thing you're allowed to criticize is the weather.

If the person you address answers in a monosyllable or less, maybe he or she is even shyer than you are. Keep smiling and move on to someone who may be more talkative.

When a group of people are having a conversation about the event, you're allowed to interject to agree with someone:

"I was thinking that too. This year's Guest Of Honor is fascinating."

Being Nice To Be Near

Flatulence never improved a relationship. There is an effective anti-gas product called "Beano" that every woman should carry on her person. Throw away the "Beano" container, put the pills in another jar, say a chromium picolinate jar, and take one before meals when dining out. If your date expresses curiosity, say "Chromium picolinate helps to metabolize sugar." Which is true.

Floss your teeth at least once a day, but never in the presence of any other human being, especially me.

Diplomacy

When visiting someone's house, do not open a closed door. If you need the bathroom, ask your hosts where it is and follow directions carefully.

Don't open their medicine chest either. Your hosts may have filled it with marbles to alert them about nosy guests.

When borrowing a friend's computer, don't click on "Favorites." They may be porn sites and are none of your business.

Don't point your finger at people unless you're singling them out for something wonderful. "*You* are the new Miss USA." or "*You* get to play the love scene with Brad Pitt."

But you *may* point with your hand, palm up.

When talking to a married couple, always address yourself to the wife, especially if the man is attractive. If the people are black, don't look at the man at all. Give him the briefest of polite nods and focus on the wife only, standing as far away from him as possible. Better to be thought autistic than have the woman think you're making eyes at her man.

If the male half of a couple gives you that fond look; you know the one I mean, the look that says "Just wait till I drop Kirsten off home, then I'll tell her I'm going out for chewing tobacco and meet you later." simply regard him opaquely, like you have no idea what he's getting at. Don't receive what he's transmitting and you just may stay out of trouble.

If you want to get into their social circle, the wife is your entree, not the husband, who just wants to rip you off for some easy sex and never see you again.

Fielding Compliments

The inability to accept a compliment gracefully discourages them and gives the impression that you've never received any before.

When one of your many admirers tells you you're pretty, you should simply smile (which makes you even prettier) and say, "Thank you." Beautiful women who hear compliments all the time have learned that this is the most appropriate response. Certainly do *not* tell the admirer how you *got* pretty and dispel the magic.

"I've been starving myself to get into this dress,... spent all afternoon at the body shop,... my sister's lipstick."

And there are different ways to deal with the several varieties of compliments. The hyperbolic one, for example. When a man avers that you are more beautiful than any entrant in the Miss Universe Pageant, you would look like seven kinds of fool if you seemed to believe it. But don't bristle and contradict him either. Just smile ever graciously and say, "Thank you. That's very flattering." Which it is.

When your admirer praises something other than your natural self, like your dress or hairdo, smile for that one too and say, "Thank you. I'm glad you like it." Then shut up!

Don't ever argue with a compliment. And most important, don't tell jokes on yourself of the "My thighs are so big that..." kind. These could give you a plain-girl aura even if you're a timeless sex goddess.

Some stand-up comics are paid a fortune to tell "I'm so ugly that..." jokes. But all you could realize from the self put-down would be pity. So if you're brimming with caustic wit, find another subject.

How about, "My ex-husband is so ugly that..."

CHAPTER TWENTY-FIVE: THE PRIVILEGE TO BE FEMALE

In closing, let's discuss some of the glorious advantages of femaleness.

As a woman, you make friends with people of both sexes more easily than a man does. Males tend to encapsulate themselves in their own egos and erect an emotional barrier to other males. But they let down this guard for a woman because you are not seen as a rival for territory. They will confide to you their hopes and fears in the expectation of getting their egos stroked in return.

Other women are more approachable too, because you're not a threat to them. This ability to find friends and make contacts everywhere gives you an entree while traveling that men don't enjoy. An attractive woman in her prime can more easily cross lines of class and lifestyle than a man can. You can date any type of person and fit in almost anywhere. So spend Thursday evening at a champagne brunch at the French Embassy and Friday afternoon riding in a pick-up truck with the cutest cow farmer in the county.

Men are so dumb that:

You know how a young man can lift up a straight-backed chair with his thing and carry it across the room? Well, some men have the muscle cut that allows them to do that, just so their things will droop down and look bigger in the locker room! It certainly doesn't work better for intercourse. This is a grotesque mutilation they undergo just to impress other guys at the gym!

Here's another example. My local TV station often shows ads for "natural male enhancement" pills which, for some reason, are set in a northeastern subdivision in the year nineteen

223

sixty-two. The narrator introduces a really goofy-looking soul called "Bob" who, it seems, has improved his outlook, delighted his wife, and impressed his neighbors since he has been using this product that promises to increase the size of his organ. "Bob" just stands still and grins like an idiot while all around him admire his purported proportions. The commercials are certainly not going to show us the actor's penis, which I would bet is quite unremarkable, so the width of his grin has to stand in for the length of his member. But some men are actually fooled into ordering, paying for, and using this ridiculous concoction.

Men are allowed very little in the way of camouflage. They may have no more than a toupee. (Which confers only on its *wearer* the illusion of having hair.)

But you can use cosmetics, fancy dresses, jewelry and flattering hairstyles to make yourself a glamorous presence. Even if you started out as a ringer for Ed Asner.

There is not so much pressure on you as on your brother to acquire wealth and status. You won't be considered a failure if you just fritter away your life planning parties, so long as you plan with style.

You can have sex with men as young and handsome as you like no matter how old and ugly you get. Though you may have to get them drunk first.

You may cry any time you feel like it.

You get to see rich and powerful men naked if you want. (And most of them look funny. Ha ha.)

You never have to undergo an examination for prostate health.

Unlike men, we have a special little organ that was created for only one purpose, pleasure. We also have a vagina for procreative access and a urethra for urinating. Males have to settle for a primitive three-in-one apparatus constructed for sexual pleasure, procreation and urination which eventually, with age, will lose all three functions. Our equipment is operational as long as we want it to be.

And the clitoris has twice as many nerve endings as a penis

in a much smaller, more manageable space. That's reason enough to be glad you chose the female side of life.

Use your natal gift of female energy to work toward your own goals and to nurture the world around you, whether or not you ever allow a lucky man to take the journey with you.

***